In *Why I Still Belie*  ney as a believer and Christian apol............ l help you grow in your faith and u............ led with uncertainty, the ugliness of hypocrisy, or the ever-present problem of pain and suffering, this book will help you understand the "messy" nature of life as a Christian from the perspective of a winsome and thoughtful defender of the faith.

> **J. Warner Wallace,** *Dateline*-featured cold-case detective, senior fellow at the Colson Center for Christian Worldview, adjunct professor of apologetics at Biola, author of *Cold-Case Christianity*, and creator of the *Case Makers Academy for Kids*

This book is Mary Jo at her most personal—witty, smart, genuine. She walks her readers through the story of her conversion to Christianity after having grown up in a thoroughly nonreligious West Coast culture . . . and afterward the shock of being hit by a host of second thoughts, doubts, and questions. She describes the secular claims and counterclaims she found herself having to work through after her conversion and gives insight into the personal challenges of encountering church culture for the first time as an adult, surprised by its frequent small-mindedness and anti-intellectualism. Mary Jo gives an honest, even raw, account of the doubts and questions even Christians may still have and guides them through to real answers.

> **Nancy Pearcey,** author of *Total Truth* and *Love Thy Body*

Why I Still Believe is a masterfully written book. Mary Jo shares her journey from atheist to influential apologist, and many of the lessons she learns along the way. It's a fun, unique, and thought-provoking book.

> **Sean McDowell,** PhD, professor at Biola University, author or coauthor of over eighteen books, including *Evidence that Demands a Verdict*

Mary Jo Sharp tells her fascinating Christian story with candor and color. Hers is a pilgrimage of bold, no-nonsense exploration—one that is filled with honest questions, frank conversations, and a spirit of wonder. She reminds us that a thoughtful faith in Christ can withstand severe scrutiny as well as open our lives to new horizons and paths of delight.

Paul Copan, Pledger Family Chair of Philosophy
and Ethics, Palm Beach Atlantic University, and
author of A *Little Book for New Philosophers*

If you've ever been hurt or disappointed by the church, then you'll relate to Mary Jo Sharp's candid account. If you're looking for inspiration to move past your pain and keep growing in your faith, then you'll love her redemptive journey. This book is unflinchingly honest; unfailingly hopeful.

Mark Mittelberg, best-selling author of *Becoming
a Contagious Christian* and *The Questions Christians
Hope No One Will Ask (With Answers)*

I am grateful for Mary Jo's friendship and her willingness to tackle tough questions and wrestle them through to a biblical solution. I also know, after having grown up in the church and having been a pastor's wife for almost four decades, that the church is not perfect. But the church is the bride of Christ, and he is perfecting her and getting her ready for his return. Join Mary Jo as she journeys through the pain of imperfect people to the only perfect one—Jesus Christ! I too still believe!

Donna Gaines, pastor's wife, Bellevue Baptist Church,
Memphis, Tennessee, and author, Bible teacher

Mary Jo was my graduate student, so the minute her story arrived, I began consuming it. Then I saw the chapter title, "Lessons from a Sociopath and an Ex-Muslim." Wow! Now who's going to stop, especially since both fellows were also grad students? Well, I was not disappointed. Try to stop reading. A new world will open before your eyes.

Gary R. Habermas, distinguished research professor
and chair, department of philosophy, Liberty University

I meet many people who are attracted to Jesus but are put off by the church and the behavior of Christians. *Why I Still Believe* is a powerful and honest response to that challenge. Mary Jo Sharp weaves together her powerful story of her own journey from atheism to faith with the stumbling blocks that Christians sometimes put in her way. Unafraid of facing real issues head on, but always responding with generosity, grace, and hope, *Why I Still Believe* is a challenge to the church to do better, a fascinating insight into a skeptic's journey to Christ, and a great resource for friends who are drawn to Jesus but suspicious of those who bear his name.

Dr. Andy Bannister, director, Solas Centre
for Public Christianity and adjunct speaker,
Ravi Zacharias International Ministries

WHY I STILL BELIEVE

A FORMER ATHEIST'S RECKONING
WITH THE BAD REPUTATION
CHRISTIANS GIVE A GOOD GOD

MARY JO SHARP

Z ZONDERVAN®

ZONDERVAN

Why I Still Believe
Copyright © 2019 by Mary Jo Sharp

Requests for information should be addressed to:
Zondervan, *3900 Sparks Dr. SE, Grand Rapids, Michigan 49546*

Zondervan titles may be purchased in bulk for educational, business, fundraising, or promotional use. For information, please email SpecialMarkets@Zondervan.com

ISBN 978-0-310-35386-7 (softcover)

ISBN 978-0-310-35389-8 (audio)

ISBN 978-0-310-35388-1 (ebook)

Some names and identifying details have been changed to protect the privacy of individuals.

Published in association with the literary agency of Mark Sweeney & Associates, Naples, Florida 34113.

Cover design: James W. Hall IV
Cover photo: gruizza/Getty Images
Interior design: Denise Froehlich

Printed in the United States of America

19 20 21 22 23 LSC 10 9 8 7 6 5 4 3 2 1

This book is dedicated to all the Treebeards,
who find no one on their side.

IN MEMORY OF

My dad, Robert Prall, 1938–2016
My friend, Nabeel Qureshi, 1983–2017

———————————

"Well, here at last, dear friends, on the shores of the Sea comes the end of our fellowship in Middle-earth. Go in peace! I will not say: do not weep; for not all tears are an evil."

—Gandalf the White, *The Return of the King*

CONTENTS

ACKNOWLEDGMENTS

This story would never have seen the light of day had there not been encouragement all along the way. From the first editor, John Sloan, who sought me out to write the book, to my agent, Mark Sweeney, who continually championed my work as I learned the ropes, to Stephanie Smith and all my Zondervan editors who took me under their wings, I owe you many thanks. To those graduate students from Houston Baptist University who video-chatted and discussed this book in its early development, I am indebted. To my readers who took time out of their busy schedules to help me find a path, you are guiding lights. To the last-minute editors, Lenny Esposito and Hillary Morgan Ferrer, who skillfully slashed and trimmed as well as offered great criticism, you have made me better. To my professors and colleagues who helped with the material, you are invaluable. To my friends, who didn't see me for months on end, you are my reprieve. And to my family who fed me, cried with me, pushed me, told me to take breaks, and prayed like there was no tomorrow . . . your crazy love truly reflects the reality of Christ's redemption.

A COSMIC ORPHAN

Have you ever zoomed out—I mean *really* zoomed out—from your life to wonder: what am I doing here? What is my life really all about?

Carl Sagan, the science popularizer from the late 1970s and 1980s, once said that the earth is but a pale, blue dot in a "great, enveloping cosmic dark."[1] We are but a single pixel in a vast universe. Words such as these weaved a backdrop upon which my childhood beliefs were formed. I never thought of being created or what it meant to transcend my personal moment-by-moment existence. Everything was focused on my insignificant existence in the vast universe. What did it really matter what I said or did? To whom, other than my parents and a relatively few others, was

---

1   Carl Sagan, *Pale Blue Dot: A Vision of the Human Future in Space* (New York: Random House, 1994), 7. This particular quote is too late to be a childhood influencer, but it represents earlier phrases that molded my childhood views.

I really accountable? These are the questions that began to rise in my later teenage years.

My family moved to Portland, Oregon, when I was two years old. My father had received the position of assistant brew master for a local start-up beer label, Henry Weinhard's Private Reserve. Once we moved, Mom and Dad decided we would never leave the Pacific Northwest because of its great beauty: the mountainous coastline with mile after mile of rocky, sandy beaches, the snow-capped volcanic peaks of the Cascade Range, the lush fern-covered rainforests, the clear-watered lakes and rivers, and the seemingly endless number of waterfalls. It was a nature lover's dream! They took my brother, sister, and me camping all up and down the Washington and Oregon coasts in a bright orange 1974 Volkswagen pop-top camper van, teaching us to love nature. Looking back at pictures of us, we look like the template for modern-day hipsters.

Though my parents raised me on a steady diet of nature and science shows, music and artistic events, camping and enjoyment of the outdoors and sports, I lacked any significant training in the deeper things of humanity: theology, philosophy, and psychology. I wasn't trained in how to think well or made aware that I should think well. So I focused on the basic American teenage pursuits: sports, music, school, and relationships. But nagging thoughts intruded on that self-centeredness. *Is this really all there is—I live and I die? Does my life even really matter? Who says it matters—my parents, my boyfriend? To be honest, they are just as insignificant in a vast universe as I am.*

I was raised in a loving, caring home, an environment ripe for my daydreaming and wondering, but my parents also liked to discuss politics. Coming from parents who were on opposite ends of the political spectrum, I witnessed a lot of engaging discussions. These conversations opened me up to thinking on the deeper things of life. I rarely settled for an answer given to me in haste or for expediency; for example, as a child, "'Cause I'm the parent, that's why" was the equivalent of throwing down the gauntlet! My dad frequently teased me that I was born a lawyer due to my love of arguing. Yet it wasn't really argument I loved. Rather, it was something I couldn't express in my limited teenage experience. I now think I was in love with the transcendent. And my strongest connection to that love was through music.

Music provided me a language through which I did not need to use words to express myself. It was a glorious liberation to find another "plane" on which I could "talk." Sitting in the middle of a band, performing a great work, released my soul into the blend of the community surrounding me. I found peace and comfort as well as drama and meaning there. However, I discovered something I never intended to find. For in the middle of a wash of musical sound, I heard the calling of the transcendent. This moment of musical beauty had to mean something. It is not for nothing that we bare our souls to create a unique experience of reflection and joy.

How fitting it was, then, that the first person to broach the subject of belief in God with me was my high school band director. In my senior year of high school, my band director gave me a graduation gift. The gift entailed two items of significance. The first item was the conducting baton he had used for my symphonic band's performance at the state concert band competition, at which we received first place that year. The award is the musical world equivalent of being state football champions. It was his first year to achieve this high honor, and so the gift of the baton was a personal sacrifice on his part. The second item was a New International Version One-Year Bible. He handed it to me and said, "When you go off to college, you're going to have hard questions. I hope you'll turn to this."

For the sake of the story, I wish I had some poignant reaction to share with you. However, the reality was a monotone response consisting of "Oh, thanks," which is, I'm sure, not what my band director expected. I didn't know what to say, but I didn't want to be rude. This second gift was highly unexpected, because he had not been evangelistic with me in any discernible way.

My band director was right: I *had* been thinking on some difficult questions of my meaning, purpose, and value in the universe, and he gave me that Bible at a time when I needed it and was likely to read it. And as I began to read, I realized I knew nothing about Christianity. This was not the goofy portrayal of Christians found on *The Simpsons* or the piously romanticized view of clergy found in old movies. Those portrayals were shallow and flat-out odd. Rather, what I was reading had substance and flesh. It was weighty and explanatory. It was history-centered, instructional, corporate, and personal. It was then and now.

I went off to college determined to go to church and find out more about Jesus. From reading through the NIV One-Year Bible (I read it faster than its one-year plan), I had come to believe that there was a God. Yet I wasn't all the way to trusting in Jesus for my salvation. Rather, I was terrified that I might be morally accountable to a Being powerful enough to create the universe. From watching years of science shows, I had some initial understanding about the kind of energy displayed by stars like our sun. I also knew of stars that greatly eclipsed the power of our sun! What if God existed as a moral being, and I was accountable to him? I felt moments of dread for my moral failings. But I didn't come to believe in God out of fear.

I went to several churches before I attended one that told me straight up why human beings need a savior. The pastor explained the original good creation and the present fallen status of humankind. As I listened, I began to piece together the concepts of good and evil and of why I seem to do the things I don't want to do. I began to understand that if humankind is the problem, then humankind is not the answer. Rather, the answer would transcend us. The Christian views made sense to me. The transcendence that had been calling me through musical beauty was God, the source of beauty and goodness himself. My conversion wasn't an emotional turnaround or a weepy moment. It was clarity, vision. I had found the transcendent to which I had been called. In my sophomore year of college, when that pastor visited my apartment to ask if I was ready to make a commitment to Jesus for my salvation, I matter-of-factly stated, "Yes, I'm ready for that now."

Some people talk of the euphoria they experienced in the moment of salvation; mine was not so much euphoric as it was a feeling of finality of commitment. It was the end of one long journey and the beginning of an even longer one. I was ready to take on the world, to soar, to find transcendent beauty, to step into fellowship with all these people who had found the good and true God.

If only I had known what was coming.

The chapters that follow are snapshots of my experience in the church and how those experiences shaped me and my beliefs. If you feel the ever-present tension of the beauty of salvation alongside the ugliness of human hypocrisy and evil, you're not alone. If you are uncomfortable in the church but feel the risk of commitment calling, this book is for you. It is for those who've wondered if they've been left a cosmic orphan, and wondered again if there's more to this unshakeable longing to belong. I can't promise any tidy endings, but there's still an irresistible Hope.

CHAPTER 1

IN THE BEGINNING
WAS . . . HYPOCRISY

> I'm not thinking so much of the historical failures of the church—inquisitions, crusades, burning people at the stake, and the like—as of personal experiences with hypocrisy, legalism, intolerance, and other besetting sins within the body of believers.
>
> **—DANIEL TAYLOR, *THE SKEPTICAL BELIEVER***

"Hey, Roger, does this dress make me look fat?"

"Um, what?"

I laughed. I was just having a bit of fun to calm my nerves. "Seriously, is this dress okay for church?"

"Yes, it's fine. You look great. You always look great. You are a fine-looking woman."

"All right, stop laying it on so thick. I'm serious. I don't know what to wear."

19

"You're making too much of this. Your dress is fine . . . and so are you." Roger gazed at me with his deep brown eyes, smiled, and walked back into the bathroom to finish tying his tie.

It was my first Sunday attending church as a Christian. Though my husband, Roger, grew up in church, it was an odd situation for me. I'd grown up without church and in a culture that wasn't overtly Christian. I'd had a few experiences with church in my youth, but it was definitely a culture of which I had little understanding. The combination of discomfort and excitement caused my thoughts to churn. I couldn't wait to get going and yet I was nervous. And as I got ready in our apartment that morning, my mind raced with uncertainties. *What should I wear? How do I act? Will people accept me? What does Roger think of all this? What would my family and friends back home think of me?*

Not too long ago, one of Roger's old girlfriends had invited Roger and me to her small Baptist church. We went and filled out a visitor's card. Shortly afterwards, the pastor came to our apartment to talk with us. We hit it off pretty quickly with this slender but rugged old Baptist preacher. Yet, even more importantly, we met right when I was at a point of making the next step in my investigation into Jesus, the step of that final commitment of belief. The pastor invited us back to the church and encouraged me to make my profession of Christ public at the church. He also encouraged me to get active in church so I could begin learning about my faith. That's why Roger and I were going to church: to become active in a faith community.

As we drove the short distance to the church, my emotions were a mess. I imagined we were about to encounter people living out beautiful, life-giving truth. But for me, church commitment was an entrance into a foreign environment, a new culture. And having come from Oregon, I was already experiencing culture shock living now in Oklahoma. Not only did my new home lack public transportation, small coffee houses and cafes, nature parks, and artsy local shops, it also lacked outdoor activities because of its extreme weather. Oklahoma in the 1990s was like living in a time warp.[1] Further, the people were way more religious[2] and much less private about their lives. It seemed like nearly everyone I met went to church! Approaching the church, I began to feel all the awkwardness of the "new kid in class." You want the other kids to like you, but you don't know what to expect. And in this case, I truly was a neophyte in the matter of spiritual things.

As we entered the church, we spotted the pastor's wife greeting people. With Roger at my side, I approached her with expectation and awkwardness. I had become a Christian the week before. However, I was going to show that commitment publicly today during the invitation time of the service. I couldn't wait for the release of all these apprehensions. I couldn't wait to be welcomed into the church community.

The pastor's wife had positioned herself so that everyone had to pass by her to get to the sanctuary. As usual, when nervous, I became an overcompensating extrovert. With a super upbeat, sing-song voice, I said, "Good morning." As she welcomed us with a smile, I noticed her sizing up my outfit. Her smile quickly

---

1 In hindsight, I enjoyed raising my daughter in Oklahoma due to that very time warp.

2 For a long time, Oregon has been considered one of the least religious states in America. In fact, "Oregon in 1952 showed the lowest rate of religious participation in the country," according to Raymond D. Gastil, "The Pacific Northwest as a Cultural Region," *The Pacific Northwest Quarterly* 64.4 (October 1973): 151, https://www.jstor.org/stable/40489715.

faded as she blurted out, "You need to find better clothes, something that doesn't show cleavage."

It took a moment to realize what she had said. *Better clothes, cleavage . . . wake up, dummy. You've just been criticized and embarrassed. I had chosen the best of my two dresses (we were poor). Wasn't that the correct choice for church? Besides . . . where was my "welcome to Jesus" moment?*

About to publicly share the biggest decision of my life, I did not expect to be greeted with a comment on my clothing. I looked down at my dress, trying to understand how its conservative neckline was showing cleavage. *Maybe I missed something. Maybe this is horribly inappropriate. No, no, you didn't. And no, no, it isn't. This is ridiculous, and it feels violating.*

Anger began to brew somewhere deep in my body, but it was still tangled up with the anticipation of the morning. I searched for a suitable reply, but nothing came. Roger made some apologetic statement, thanked her for pointing out the issue, and ushered me into the sanctuary. My first worship experience as a Christian had been sufficiently corrupted. The rest of the morning, I forced a smile.

Roger and I reacted to the incident very differently. He put trust and authority in the church leaders and made adjustments accordingly. I had the opposite reaction. The encounter immediately raised distrust in me toward these church leaders. I don't remember the sermon that day. My mind was still busy working through the incident. *You are reading too much into her statement. It was a bad choice on her part, and you don't know why she said that. How would you like it if people judged your character for your one-time decision to eat lemon sherbet ice cream with chocolate sprinkles?*

Although I agreed with my own assessment, I have to admit

that a seed of doubt germinated in me that very day. I have always been a glass-half-empty kind of person, so it was typical of me to distrust. But how I wish someone had warned me not to get my hopes up. *First-time church attendance should come with a disclaimer. Churches could post a sign or place fine print at the bottom of the bulletin: "Church attendance may cause extreme discomfort. Side effects of interactions with humans include, but are not limited to, doubt, anger, disappointment, and disillusionment."*

Even so, it would take more than one thoughtless comment to disrupt my commitment. I did walk down the aisle that day and make a public profession of my faith in Jesus. It was awkward. Since I came from a culture that is more private about our beliefs, walking down in front of everyone felt forced and showy. Plus, I was understandably self-conscious about my dress. However, I'm not one to back down once I put my mind to something. Not only did I walk that aisle, but I stood in the foyer after the service with the pastor next to me while people came by and greeted me.

The next week, I was baptized and became a member of the church. *Hold on . . . you're going to join that church? Are you crazy?* Honestly, I didn't know anything about church. I wouldn't have thought to check out other churches. Everything was so different, awkward, and new that I didn't even really think through the whole situation. I was a college student, living halfway across the country from my family, and I was a new mother. There was a lot going on in my mind and in my life. So I was counting on my husband to lead on this matter since he grew up in church.

For the first two months of church, I enrolled in a discipleship class on prayer life. The leader of the course was an elderly woman who had a gentle and patient spirit. That class was a much-needed encouragement and a counterbalance to the pastor's wife. After those two months, I became involved with ministry by volunteering in the youth program. Roger also began volunteering about halfway through that first year. When our youth minister suddenly gave his two-weeks' notice, the church looked to Roger to lead the youth ministry part-time. He eventually became a full-time minister. And I can now say that I did not know "trouble" until my family got involved in ministry.

While I wasn't naive enough to expect everyone in the church to be an angel, nor ministry to be painless, I didn't expect what was to come. The church had its self-named watch guards who zealously defended their cultural choices for worship style, dress, and so on, even when they had no theological basis for doing so. Many times, these guardians unknowingly (and perhaps knowingly too) twisted Scripture to defend their preferences. During our first church ministry, we endured full-blown attacks on our character or ministry choices, all of which shocked me, having come from a much more accepting environment.

No one who has been in ministry for very long will be surprised at this behavior by church members. It's unfortunately common. However, in addition to handling the drama of the church, my husband and I lived below the poverty line, with a baby, in a run-down apartment in a very challenging neighborhood—while trying to finish up college, hold part-time jobs, and minister full-time. Through my husband's ministry, we had grown the youth group to one-third the size of the total church membership. After five years with no health insurance, and nearing bankruptcy, we had to move on to another church to survive.

In our second church, my husband took on a dual position of worship pastor and youth minister. The dual position was much more demanding, due to the constant attention needed in both ministries. Plus, at this point Roger was a novice in worship ministry. However, the new church had just built a sanctuary with a more contemporary design, and the search committee had specifically chosen Roger to help them move in a more modern direction with worship. So we were excited to find a church that seemed to want to minister to a changing culture. However, our excitement was short-lived. While many of the volunteers and staff members were welcoming and encouraging, some of the parishioners were less so.

For example, after one of my husband's first Sundays leading worship in our new church, a short, stout woman marched up the center aisle. Her dress suit gave her the shape of a refrigerator box, and her hair was tightly coiffed in short, dark curls. Her facial expression matched her rigid appearance. Her husband, a church deacon, was waiting in the foyer, just out of our range of sight. I smiled as she approached Roger and me, since many church members were still introducing themselves and welcoming us. Without so much as an introduction or a greeting, however, the woman blurted out: "I don't know what god you're worshiping up there." Apparently, she did not like the more contemporary musical selections.

There was a moment of thick, heavy silence. Having expected a warm word of welcome, I was caught off guard. That little old lady had just blindsided us with a full Chuck Norris roundhouse blow. My heart sank. *Here we go again.*

My husband, tough as he is, was still vulnerable in his new ministry position, and I had no idea how he was going to take this attack. However, I had gotten my fill of such behavior at our last church and wasn't going to put up with any more nonsense. My whole body lurched forward as I offered up my own ninja-style retort: "Well, it better be the same God as you *or it's the devil!*"

The words came out before I even knew what I was saying,

but I honestly didn't regret what I had said. I was already distrustful of people in the church because of our previous experiences. Not only did many people seem to lack consideration for our newness in ministry, but many had also showed little concern for our family's impoverished situation.

Roger thrust his arm in front of me to coax me backward as he began to engage the deacon's wife. "So, June, what is your concern with the music?"

"Those songs you sang. We don't like them. In fact, we hate them. They aren't appropriate for church."

"What do you mean that they aren't appropriate?"

"The music is loud and has too much drum. We can't hear the organ."

"You can't hear the organ? Well, I can help with that. Do you not like the drums or were they too loud?"

"Church hymns don't need drums. They belong in a rock band."

"Oh, okay, I think I understand. You don't like the more contemporary feel. Was there anything about the music that was a theological issue?"

"We just don't like those 7–11 songs." Her statement was a derogatory church colloquialism. It meant singing the same seven words eleven times.

I couldn't believe the conversation that was unfolding. *Really? Are we really having a conversation of the 1980s in a church of the 2000s?* Back in the 1980s, one of the biggest battlegrounds in the church was over worship style. Hadn't we moved past that?

My frustration level skyrocketed. *What universe had I entered? Why were church people concerned with the least-concerning issues?* No one marched down the aisle to complain that we weren't representing Christ well in our community, or that we weren't learning the Bible at a deep enough level. Nobody called attention to the fact that our nearly all-white, middle-class church didn't look like the actual body of Christ or that we weren't paying enough attention to the sick and needy.

One after another, everything I perceived as wrong with the church marched into my mind. And then came the lament, a mix of homesickness and sick-of-church-ness: *I can't believe I gave up the Northwest for this Southern-brewed batch of hypocrisy.*

My disgust kept fermenting as we packed up our things and got into the car. "How can she call herself a Christian?" I asked.

Roger looked at me, eyebrows raised, but let me continue.

"I'm just so sick of the church acting as though they are truly followers of Christ, when, in fact, they do mean-spirited stuff like this and lack even the smallest concern for the biggest issues. She should know better. She's been a Christian too long to act that way. She should be mentoring us. She should not be someone we have to correct on basic things such as 'how not to be a total jerk.' No wonder people leave the church. They are a massive bunch of hypocrites who care more about their favorite song being sung than about actually knowing Jesus Christ."

"Jo, you're going too far with this whole thing. She's just being a bit immature. It's not worth getting upset about."

"Too far? Too far? She called you a devil worshiper! And that's the problem. The people who've been Christians forever should be at least *a little* mature. I can't believe someone who has made it this far in their Christian life lacks basic manners. Besides, we are new here and you're brand new to music ministry. Why in the world would she think that it was a Christian action to demonize someone who's just starting out in worship ministry? It makes no sense . . . unless she's not a Christian, or just a person who thinks she's a Christian. Doesn't she have a conscience? Shouldn't the Holy Spirit be telling her 'Nooooooo, June, nooooo.'"

Roger shook his head. "You're making definitive claims on her Christianity. But we can't say that about her."

I looked at Roger, irritated and speechless. *You're arguing for her now? What? She just lambasted you in front of the church!*

"Just because she doesn't like the music doesn't mean she's not a Christian," he said.

That's not what I'm arguing.

"Besides, it's not really worth our time to fight about it."

Oh no, you didn't just say that. Did Roger really think this argument wasn't worth it? June was a deacon's wife! She was supposed to be a leader in the church. And we hadn't even officially met her. Yet here she was, attacking us on our very first encounter!

I wasn't just angry about one incident; I was despairing that we had left a ridiculous situation in one church only to immediately find ridiculousness in another. In my anger, I wasn't explaining myself well. At the time, in my mid-twenties, I barely knew how to express all that was bothering me. June was just one more representative of the lack of loving tact and self-control I encountered overall in the people who called themselves "the church."

I had initially been drawn to the church because of the great beauty and goodness I found in creation and then in the Scriptures. In John 13:34–35 Jesus taught, "A new commandment I give to you, that you love one another: just as I have loved you, you also are to love one another. By this all people will know that you are my disciples, if you have love for one another." Later, John reports Jesus praying for the believers who were to come (that's us), "that they may become perfectly one, so that the world may know that you sent me and loved them even as you

loved me" (John 17:23). Paul emphasized how we are supposed
to accomplish such oneness: "Do nothing from selfish ambition
or conceit, but in humility count others more significant than
yourselves. Let each of you look not only to his own interests, but
also to the interests of others" (Philippians 2:3–4). James taught
us that we are to be quick to hear, slow to speak, and slow to anger
(James 1:19). He also pointed out that "those who consider themselves religious and yet do not keep a tight rein on their tongues
deceive themselves, and their religion is worthless" (1:26 NIV).

I loaded these passages into my brain to take to church, where
I expected to find people who believed these teachings were true
and practiced them in their daily life. Instead, too often I encountered self-focused, judgmental people who burdened themselves
with little, if any, discernible concern for their fellow believers in
Christ, let alone for the broader world. I began to suspect many
church people didn't know or believe the Bible at all.

Aggravating my encounters at church was the fact that I am
an ideologue. Just try to go to a movie with me and you'll end up
wishing you didn't. I love to figure out the writers' and director's
philosophical commitments and how those worked their way into
the characters and plotline. It can be quite annoying, especially
when I see a philosophical commitment being pushed on the
audience as if it were obviously true. I recoil at the arrogance and
lack of nuance. Now, put my personality into a church setting.
My thoughts look something like this: *Why do these people call
themselves Christian when they don't even try to follow the Word
of God? Why are they pushing their philosophy on me when they
don't even act like it's true? If they believed it, they'd live the way
it tells them to.*

This is where I wish I could go back and slap some sense into
my young self. I began to create a narrative in my mind that *I was*

committed to the truth, but that the church was obviously more committed to her cultural traditions. It is hard to understand exactly why this dichotomy became my story. I was definitely hurting from the disappointment of glaring hypocrisy which led to ruinous encounters. And I'm pretty sure I was well entrenched in post-Enlightenment thinking that continued to goad my skepticism. However, I was also not considering Scripture where Jesus and the apostle Paul dealt with hypocrisy among believers (Matthew 7:3–5; Romans 2:24).

I began to see myself as the noble truth seeker who had only the desire to figure out if Christianity was true. All the while, I had little awareness that I was growing in emotional rebellion, a rebellion in which truth seeking was increasingly warped with emotion. I wanted out of the church. I despised that I was subtly expected to look, act, and think like a Southern evangelical woman when I was raised in a strikingly different culture. I despaired that no one cared to know me deeply. I cringed at the lack of intellectual challenge in the church. And I hated how arrogant that previous sentiment sounded. I lamented how wrapped up in myself I had become.

The result of my brewing rebellion was that I wanted to find a way out. I had already begun to stack the deck against Christianity, even while unaware I was doing so. I had all sorts of rationalizations for why the church was full of people who didn't really believe and who were anti-intellectual: (1) They cared more about a person's clothing than their soul. (2) The style of songs we sung in worship was more important to a person's Christianity than learning about and knowing God. (3) Sports seemed more valuable to students, their parents, and the pastors than was discipleship. (4) No one ever discussed whether Christianity was true; they just made assumptions. (5) Outside of attending church, the average professing Christian I encountered looked not much different than the average nonprofessing person in general lifestyle choices and habits.

Most of my agnostic and atheist friends I had known growing up were more pleasant and thoughtful people than I encountered in the church. I remember telling Roger, "Well, no wonder the church is losing people. . . we create atheists right here in church!"

David Kinnaman, a sociologist, reports in his book *UnChristian*:

> In virtually every study we conduct, representing thousands of interviews every year, born-again Christians fail to display much attitudinal or behavioral evidence of transformed lives. For instance, based on a study released in 2007, we found that most of the lifestyle activities of born-again Christians were statistically equivalent to those of non-born-agains. When asked to identify their activities over the last thirty days, born-again believers were just as likely to bet or gamble, to visit a pornographic website, to take something that did not belong to them, to consult a medium or psychic, to physically fight or abuse someone, to have consumed enough alcohol to be considered legally drunk, to have used an illegal, nonprescription drug, to have said something to someone that was not true, to have gotten back at someone for something he or she did, and to have said mean things behind another person's back.[3]

The problem of hypocrisy has huge consequences for the perception of Christians:

3 David Kinnaman, *UnChristian: What a New Generation Really Thinks about Christianity . . . and Why It Matters* (Grand Rapids: Baker, 2007), 47, Kindle.

Here is what all of this boils down to—and, I believe, one of the most important findings of our research for this book: among young outsiders, 84 percent say they personally know at least one committed Christian. Yet just 15 percent thought the lifestyles of those Christ followers were significantly different from the norm. This gap speaks volumes.[4]

The statistics represent my experience in church. What I found in the church was a bunch of superficially polite people who were very much lacking in personal introspection and self-discipline, theological depth, philosophical intelligence, and sacrificially loving friendships. Of course, the entire church wasn't this way, but as I sometimes do, I began to "wholesale" the situation. I accumulated all my former bad experiences with people in the church—all my hurt—and brought everything into my current circumstance.

What it all came down to was that I didn't leave my atheism in order to find a nicer environment of nice people in their culture of being polite. I could find all those things in circles of atheist friends. Instead, I was looking for a life-changing, Christ-focused community, a church family with real accountability to a transcendent and objective good that they pursued as actually true. And it was nowhere to be found. By the end of our time at that second church, my faith in people had flatlined, and my faith in God needed resuscitation.

Despite my disappointment, a sobering analogy kept coming to mind, a memory of when our daughter Emily was born. As we were getting ready to take our newborn baby home, Roger pulled the car up to the hospital door. I walked out of the hospital with

---

4 Kinnaman, *UnChristian*, 48.

Emily in my arms into a cloud of cigarette smoke. A few doctors and nurses were outside taking a smoke break. I was appalled at this scene of sheer hypocrisy, disgusted that I had to walk through this cloud of smoke with my newborn. Later, I began to understand that just because the doctors and nurses knew smoking was bad for their health didn't mean they always acted like that belief was true. In this case, they had adopted lifestyles in direct rebellion to one of the truths of their own profession.

Similarly, I knew that though people could say they believed in God, they didn't always act like it was true. Further, some of them had made choices directly opposed to the teachings of their own religion. *But what do I do about it?* As author Daniel Taylor noted,

> There is something repellent about the distortions of community as actually practiced so often in the church. The pressure for uniformity, the spirit of legalism, the use of Christianity to sanctify cultural fetishes, and a host of other problems common in the church make wholehearted participation difficult for anyone with a sense of self or low tolerance for cliché and hypocrisy.[5]

At this point, I had gained no means by which to thoughtfully handle these situations other than angry outbursts, such as, "How can these people say they believe the Bible?" Further, as a minister's wife I was not afforded space to struggle with doubt, nor could I ask hard questions. My analytical mind and interest in philosophy also isolated me from most people in our churches.

---

5   Daniel Taylor, *The Myth of Certainty: The Reflective Christian and the Risk of Commitment* (Downers Grove, IL: InterVarsity Press, 1992), 108.

I noticed an underlying distrust of me. Whenever I would ask a difficult question about belief, I was quickly brushed aside, or the subject was changed. Not surprisingly, I began to earnestly question my belief in God within the first decade of becoming a Christian. What originally began as doubt turned into intellectual questioning driven by a desire to leave the church, and Christianity, behind.

Yet something else pulled on me as well. There was something beautiful and good in what I had originally discovered about Christianity. I had discovered the source of the beauty I saw all around me: the beautiful Creator himself. I had read the stories of great love and sacrifice by Jesus and his disciples. The words and stories in the Bible expressed a reality I longed to encounter. There I saw a counterintuitive goodness: sacrifice over self-preservation, losing oneself to find oneself. These things seemed to make uncommon sense of my world, and I was drawn to them.

I was now faced with the question, "But is Christianity also true?" I could have been deceived. Perhaps my desire for an experience of beauty and goodness left me too open to finding something to fill a void. Perhaps I had believed before I understood what I was doing. When I became a Christian, I was only twenty years old, recently married, and an unexpectedly new mom. Maybe I felt lost and like I was flailing around, and so in Christianity I found a place to land. There were so many questions: *How do I know God exists? Why do I believe Jesus rose from the dead? Isn't Jesus's story just like other myths? Aren't all religions basically the same? Can religion even tell me truth?* And yet I wondered if truth ultimately mattered to me. *Does my desire to leave outweigh any reasons to stay? Do I even know what I'm asking?*

One Sunday, in that second church, I snuck into the church

library when I thought no one would be around. I was looking for a book to help me with my questions, but I didn't even know what kind of book. It took me a couple of tries, but to my surprise, I eventually found a book that looked like it might help—*The Case for Christ* by Lee Strobel. As I read, I was intrigued that the author was actually giving evidence for the truth of Christianity. Instead of just *assuming* Christianity was true, he treated Christianity as something that could be substantiated. *Well, that's refreshing!* However, since I had very little experience with doubting a worldview, I decided to remain open but skeptical. *God, you're going to have to show me you're real, because I'm not seeing you in your people.*

• CONSIDERATIONS •

1. Where are you currently in your search for God?
2. What experiences or people color your view of God?
3. Have you ever been in a stressful situation that caused you to have questions about God? Why did that situation cause you to begin questioning?
4. Have you begun to find answers to your questions? If not, what's keeping you from doing so?

CHAPTER 2

WEARING THE WRONG CLOTHING

If you're going to be a doubter, be sure to doubt your
doubts as well as your beliefs.

—DALLAS WILLARD

**My husband isn't good at recognizing the difference in
women's clothing sizes.** However, he is extremely thoughtful
about washing, folding, and putting away laundry. When these
two characteristics come together, it can be quite amusing. Roger
would fold the laundry and put the items in our dresser drawers.
Then, in the morning, I would open my underwear drawer and
find my preteen daughter's set of underwear staring back at me.

"Roger-dodger?"

"Yes?"

"Where are you? I need to show you something."

"I'm in the kitchen."

I sauntered into the kitchen with my daughter's underwear halfway up one leg over my clothing, a completely serious look on my face. "So, I think I'll wear these today. I found them in my drawer. What do you think?"

Roger smiled. "Oh, that's not your underwear, is it?"

"No, but I'm flattered that you think I'd fit into these."

It wasn't just an underwear issue. Roger's clothing-size judgment skills extended to all pieces of my wardrobe. Over the years, I've found my shirts in Emily's room and my jeans in Roger's closet. I routinely engage in impromptu fashion shows to demonstrate the error.

Now, suppose for a moment that I didn't recognize the error before I put an item on. Assume that I just put on the underwear and then wondered why I felt uncomfortable. For me, that is what "churchy faith" felt like. Trying to put on my church's cultural expression of faith made me feel like an imposter, like I was wearing someone else's Jesus-believing clothes. Yet I had no idea how to find a genuinely fitting faith. And so doubt began to creep into my soul.

The quite tricky part about my doubt is that it wasn't all-consuming. I could keep trudging through church ministry because doubt couldn't quickly dethrone my well-formed personality and habits, such as my people-pleasing, overachieving ways, pride, and desire to belong to a community. Though, in some ways, I wish my doubt had been more potent. If my doubt had been paralyzing, perhaps I would have had to deal with it more quickly and in a much more dramatic fashion. If I had my way, I would have been given time off to handle my doubts, and I would have tackled them one by one, logically and methodically. However, life does not work that way; it's too messy. So doubt crept into my life, crippling me slowly rather than all at once.

Every time something bad happened at church, doubt would remind me that it had been with me all along.

My ability to pinpoint the problem was as bad as Roger's ability to determine whose underwear was whose. I felt lost in this endeavor. I had no training from the church in how to handle cantankerous church people, much less how to handle doubt about God's existence stemming from those same church people. *So what if I'd read a book that gave me evidence for the claims of Christianity?* I still had concerns and questions. Further aggravating the issue, I felt caged by my circumstances, for I determined there was no person I could truly trust to discuss this matter with, especially not as a staff wife. I had yet to meet another staff wife who openly or even discreetly discussed her own concerns about the validity of the whole Christian endeavor. Plus, the few times I had opened up about serious life issues, I had been burned by the fiery arrows of gossip and marginalization. The Christians I had met so far taught me (albeit indirectly) to hide my problems and my doubts.

Looking back on that time, I realize there are three ways to approach doubt. First, to my dismay, many Christians view doubt as an enemy of faith. Second, and more helpfully, doubt can be viewed as a normal part of the maturation process. And third, doubt has an unavoidable relational aspect; doubt is not just a logical problem but a personal one. Let's take a closer look at these three ways of looking at doubt.

DOUBT AS AN ENEMY OF FAITH

I was never taught explicitly that doubt is an enemy of faith. Rather, I picked up this view from general attitudes and actions in the church. Many times when I saw teachers, leaders, or pastors challenged in Bible study classes or in small talk, I witnessed replies laden with defensive-sounding posturing, *often* covered over with a charming smile. Their defensiveness always angered me. Honestly, my church experience felt like it should have been titled "A Series of Unfortunate Events."

I once invited an atheist acquaintance, Devon, to my church for a class on Genesis (which had a young-earth focus). After the main session, the leader opened the floor for questions. Devon cautiously raised his hand and asked, "How can you reconcile modern science with a young-earth view?"

I thought Devon's question was appropriate for this topic, and especially since it came from an atheist. I'll admit, I was intrigued to hear what the leader would say in response. I knew this leader was aggressively and belligerently one-sided on this matter with no room for alternative views. In fact, he had been known to verbally berate people who did not share his opinion, without a shred of concern about how he acted. So I began to think, or rather pray, "Please be gracious, please be gracious," as I awaited the answer.

To my dismay, the leader responded, "That's just what you have to believe if you're going to take the Bible seriously. Jesus believed Genesis was true [the leader meant 'literal']. If the Old Testament is good enough for Jesus, it's good enough for me."

Oh, man. He just gave a "The Bible says it, I believe it, and that settles it" response. I wondered if he was going to expand his Genesis argument to be more robust or offer any of the objections against his argument and rebuttals to those objections. He did not do so.

Much to my surprise, Devon followed up with another question. "But didn't the early church father Augustine caution us against this kind of treatment of Genesis?"

At the time, I wasn't even aware that this current hot-topic issue could be found in Augustine's writing from the fourth century.[1] I was fascinated, wondering if Devon was quoting the passage correctly or perhaps taking it out of context.

The class leader was silent. *Please be gracious. Please be gracious.* The senior pastor, who had been sitting in the audience, immediately popped up, face rapidly flushing, and began his own lecture on how the interpretation of Genesis is connected to salvation. "If you don't believe in a young-earth view, I can't say you're not saved, but *you're wrong!* Though salvation doesn't come from believing in a literal six-day creation, it's connected." My surprise quickly devolved to horror as this Christian pastor pounced on Devon, who was obviously a guest, and who wasn't being discourteous in any way.

The pastor went back to his seat while the leader abruptly shut down questions and began lecturing again, even though it was nearing the end of the session. Before I knew what was happening, the pastor had come over to where we were sitting. He forcefully dropped a stack of magazines in Devon's lap and

---

1   My friend referenced Augustine's writing in "The Literal Meaning of Genesis," written about AD 415. Augustine appears to have the belief that the original creation happened in an instant. However, his writing on Genesis 1 has been utilized for support on all sides of the age-of-the-earth controversy. Regarding the interpretation of Genesis, Augustine said, "If they [unbelievers] find a Christian mistaken in a field which they themselves know well and hear him maintaining his foolish opinions about our books, how are they going to believe those books in matters concerning the resurrection of the dead, the hope of eternal life, and the kingdom of heaven, when they think their pages are full of falsehoods on facts which they themselves have learnt from experience and the light of reason?" (Saint Augustine, *The Literal Meaning of Genesis*, ed. Johannes Quasten, Walter J. Burghardt, and Thomas Comerford Lawler, trans. John Hammond Taylor, Ancient Christian Writers 41 [Mahwah, NJ: Paulist, 1982], 42–43).

said, "There. You can find all the answers in these." With that, the pastor turned and walked back to his seat.

No, no, no, no! How could you do that? Devon is our guest! You just reaffirmed any prejudice he might have had that Christians are intolerant hypocrites who preach love and mercy but flippantly dole out wrath and judgment. Why? Why couldn't you compassionately handle this man's doubt?

Devon sat beside me, avoiding eye contact, and then swiftly got up to leave the class. I hurried after him, heart pounding from anger and disappointment. As we walked to his car, I bumbled alongside, attempting to fix things.

"I'm so sorry for what happened back there. It was wrong of him to treat you that way."

"Mary Jo, it's not your fault."

"But I invited you and I'm honestly horrified with everything that just happened."

"Don't worry about it."

Out of my embarrassment I began to overreach. "You're always welcome to ask me a question or continue pursuing this matter with me. I'll meet you at a coffee house or you can email me."

We got to his car. Devon paused, and with an anguished look he dryly said, "Thanks." Then he got in his car and drove off, never to return, never to contact me again.

Why did this happen? Why did this Christian pastor think he had to get aggressive or angry in order to prove his point? Why was he so intimidated by this question about belief in God?

The class on Genesis had been put together by the pastor in reaction to an apologetics survey course at the church during which I taught the different models of the intersection of science and faith. In class, I didn't commit to any of the views—in part because I wasn't a pastor of the church but also because of my educational training in how to run a class discussion. The point of the survey course was to allow church members to determine their own view based on the knowledge they had, since many of them were scientists or engineers in the NASA community. In class, I discovered that church members held a variety of views about the age of the earth.

But at this church the leaders suffered from authoritarianism, a leadership style that is as destructive of human relationships as it is antithetical to the teachings of Christ. As author Daniel Taylor notes, "In environments tainted with authoritarianism, every question creates a mini crisis."[2] The pastor, and a few of his fellow church leaders, felt the class challenged their beliefs since it didn't emphasize that there was only one way to believe on this matter. At the risk of sounding disingenuous, I never thought this would be the outcome. I thought a church that was full of scientists and engineers would welcome the chance to learn about the history of the science-faith arguments, and many members of my class did so. It was quite the wake-up call to discover that the going gossip, even presented at a church-wide meeting, was that I was "not teaching the Bible as the authoritative Word of God."

It was no wonder that this situation climaxed with aggression targeting a nonchurch member. The authoritarian environment stewed such belligerence that it was only a matter of time before it reached a boiling-over point. While I understand that the age of the earth is a heated topic of debate, if Christians have nothing better to offer in how we handle disagreements than to present a culture of authoritarianism, then how would anyone see the

---

2 Daniel Taylor, *The Myth of Certainty: The Reflective Christian and the Risk of Commitment* (Downers Grove, IL: InterVarsity Press, 1992), 36.

difference that Jesus is supposed to make in our lives? Yet I don't
think their reaction was as simple as just feeling their authority
challenged on age of the earth. Within the whole framework of
this issue, there was no room for a person to question or have any
doubt. There's more going on here than just an argument over a
secondary or tertiary issue in Christianity.[3]

Author Gregory Boyd believes that, within conservative evan-
gelicalism, there is a propensity toward a certainty-seeking model
of faith, which expresses itself by viewing doubt as an enemy or
as destructive to belief in God.[4] He compares this mode of faith
with a familiar carnival game, the Strength Tester game. In the
game, your strength is tested by how hard you can swing the
mallet. In a certainty-seeking model, your faith is measured by
the intensity of your own psychological certainty—how hard you
can swing your faith mallet to send your faith puck up the pole
to get as close to the certainty bell as possible.[5]

Though I try not to shove individual personalities into an
explanatory box of why-they-are-the-way-they-are, I've frequently
encountered Christians using this approach toward doubt. Boyd's
description made a lot of sense to me. Some Christians seem to
think, *If I just express my certainty more loudly or aggressively,
if I just refuse to budge on anything I believe, or if I just ignore
the problems, then doubts will go away and I'll live the victorious*

---

3 For a brief discussion on levels of doctrinal importance, see Samuel Emadi,
"Theological Triage and the Doctrine of Creation," *The Gospel Coalition*, October
20, 2015, https://www.thegospelcoalition.org/article/theological-triage-and-the
-doctrine-of-creation/.

4 I have some theological differences with Gregory Boyd, but his work on doubt
is excellent. Therefore, I do not wish to "wholesale" this Christian thinker by rejecting all of what he says due to specific differences.

5 Gregory A. Boyd, *Benefit of the Doubt: Breaking the Idol of Certainty* (Grand
Rapids: Baker, 2013), 26, Kindle.

Christian life! However, the problem with the certainty-seeking approach is that it makes critical thinking "a supreme liability."[6] To think critically on a matter, I've got to be open to that fact that I might be wrong. If I'm wrong, my faith puck isn't going to make it all the way up to the 100 percent ring of the certainty bell, which makes life a bit more difficult. The answers aren't so easy to obtain. I can't just ring the bell and move on to the next game at the carnival. I have to learn to question and to trust.

To question my beliefs takes trust. That's the hard part for me: to trust. It takes the control away from me and hands it over to God. My ideas about him, and about life, could be very wrong, but I've learned to live in those ideas. I've become familiar with the environment my ideas have created for me to live in, and in that environment, I feel some control. Perhaps that's one of the big issues on both sides of the debate on God's existence: we want autonomy to rule over our individual lives . . . completely. I know how awful I feel when life seems to be completely out of my ability to shape it the way I desire. Yet learning to trust God means trusting him even with my mind.

It hurts to say that many of my brothers and sisters in Christ have knowingly or unknowingly demonstrated that critical thinking is a supreme liability in their lives. I can still hear the familiar phrases from the pulpit and the halls of the churches in which we served: *we have too much head knowledge, we need more heart knowledge; those ivory-tower theologians; you're thinking too hard; seminary ruins pastors; she likes to think, but I prefer to get my hands dirty; I don't read books; what good can come from philosophy?; you don't have enough faith;* etcetera ad nauseam.

Sadly, we ministered at churches that I eventually could not

---

6 Boyd, *Benefit of the Doubt*, 36.

recommend to others in good conscience due to an environment in which critical thinking was rebuked rather than celebrated. On this matter of critical thinking I tend to agree with the angry atheist, but only in part. Not all Christians make their habitat a certainty-seeking model. Yet I can see that if a person experiences enough Christians who do, that person could believe that all Christians avoid critical thinking. I was that person, living in that scenario, and at times doubt definitely felt like an enemy of faith.

DOUBT AS AN INSTRUCTIVE AND NATURAL PART OF MATURATION

Rather than viewing doubt as an enemy to faith, maybe doubt could be viewed as part of growing up. As a child, though I liked to argue, there was a time when I just trusted my parents and their authority in my life. Of course, being strong-willed, I had my moments of rebellion. For example, one time I got a punk-rock haircut after my mom told me not to. But for the most part I trusted and obeyed my parents. In my later childhood and early teenage years my knowledge of the world began to expand, and I began to have doubts about things my parents said and believed. I often questioned them or pushed back on them. My parents never assumed any ill will or lack of love as the reason for my questions. They knew that I was still young and navigating my way in the world.

I was outgrowing my old clothes of belief. My childhood faith and trust in my parents didn't fit me anymore, for I needed to develop a deeper kind of faith and trust. It was not a lack of *any* trust, just a different *kind* of trust. It was a growing, maturing faith and trust. I needed appropriately sized clothing for my current age.

To return to my earlier analogy: when I playfully paraded around the house in my daughter's clothing, I didn't expect to continue to wear that clothing the rest of the day. Neither should I want to parade around in my initial thoughts about God as I get older as a Christian. However, I *was* donning those youthful Christian belief clothes. This lack of maturing in my understanding of God made a substantial impact on me for ill.

I didn't really understand how to bring together the reality that while God's character doesn't change, mine was changing. In fact, everything around me was changing. The culture has changed since I became a Christian. Technology has changed since I became a Christian. The world has changed since I became a Christian. All these changes impacted my thoughts, ideas, and character. I am not a static being. Plus, as I've aged, I have seen much more disease, suffering, death, and evil. Ideas, such as God's goodness, that once seemed rather basic or easy to accept, now had to contend with my experiences of the wretchedness of human evil. Acceptance of God's goodness took much more understanding, and so the questions came. However, should my questioning be equated to an ill will or lack of love toward God? While I can certainly pervert or manipulate questioning in several ways, ill will is not a *necessary property* of questioning. Even Scripture reminds us to "have mercy on those who doubt" (Jude 1:22).

C. S. Lewis argued that problems arise when I begin to think that once I decide something is true I will never again have questions about that belief. Such an expectation is superficial. It lacks an understanding of the human condition. Humans are capable of doubting knowledge that they have considered by reason to be true. I understand this notion a little too well. Like Lewis, my beliefs developed from two vastly different worldviews: atheism and Christianity. At times I have romanticized my views, and my ability to reason has been undermined by my emotions and desires. *If I just go back to the simpler life of my former atheism, everything would be fine. If Christians would just behave as though the Bible were true, everything would be fine.* My own desires can mess up my reasoning, for I can rationalize[7] practically anything I want to be true. Once my passion gets involved, my reason, unassisted by grace, has a snowflake's chance in a blast furnace to hold on to truths already gained.[8]

As doubt crept into my spiritually immature mind, I did not consider that my beliefs might have been melting in the blast furnace of my own desires. Honestly, who really recognizes if something like that is happening, anyway? How odd would that internal dialog be?

> *"Self, you know, you keep saying your doubt is solely based on unanswered questions, but have you thought yet that you may just want to ditch this whole Christianity thing because of reasons unrelated to the truth of Christianity?"*

> What? No! I am smarter than that. I would know if my appetites were conquering my reason.

> *"Wow. Now you're pulling out the fancy words. You're really avoiding this possibility, aren't you?"*

---

7   I use this term here in the abused way in which it has been utilized in the late twentieth and early twenty-first century. I do not mean that I can fit anything I want to be true into a logically valid, true, and convincing argument in a formal sense of logic, but rather that I can use my reasoning abilities to persuade myself that I am correct even if I lack a valid, true, and convincing argument on my behalf.
8   Adapted from C. S. Lewis, *Christian Reflections* (San Francisco: HarperOne, 2014), 864–72, Kindle.

Of course not! I am searching for truth. I am committed to finding out whether or not this whole religion thing is worthwhile . . . I mean, evidenced and reasoned.

"Now you're just embarrassing yourself."

What do you mean? I'm the one being objective here.

"Good luck with that."

This kind of doubt can be categorized as **volitional doubt**.[9] I had to come to terms with my desire for the Christian faith to be false simply because I was disgusted with the hurtful behaviors of people in the church. I had not yet considered that there was more to the human doubt issue than just evidence and reason. We human beings are not "logic machines,"[10] as Mr. Spock declared on *Star Trek*. Many factors shape and frame my beliefs, but many factors also shape and frame my doubts.

Volitional doubt "is chiefly concerned with one's will; specifically one's willingness to believe. One characteristic of this doubt is that a person may have indicated they appreciate the evidence, while still not being able to commit to where the evidence leads. It is a matter of the will."

Gary Habermas,

Dealing with Doubt

---

9 See Gary Habermas, *Dealing with Doubt (Chicago: Moody, 1990),* available from www.garyhabermas.com/books/dealing_with_doubt/dealing_with_doubt.htm.

10 John Ortberg, *Faith and Doubt* (Grand Rapids: Zondervan, 2008), Kindle edition, 71–72.

DOUBT AS RELATIONAL

Perhaps one of the more difficult problems with my questioning was that my doubt was directed toward a person, and I was basically unaware of it. My doubt had beginnings in distrust of people, human persons who professed allegiance and submission to another kind of *person*. In hindsight, I can see that my distrust of Christians had transferred to distrust of Jesus. I had experienced poor relationships, authoritarian leadership, and anti-intellectualism from the outset of my commitment to a local church body. I had very little Christian relational influence upon which to model my relational trust of God. It's like people who can't believe in God the Father because they themselves experienced a bad father. (Ironically, I had a good father, who generally didn't mention God unless he was telling a particularly funny joke.) However, if asked, I would have told you that I was interested solely in discovering what was true. Unlike "those" people who had grown up in church, I had no background in Christianity, no commitments I had to uphold. I could see with the dry light of objectivity.

Can you see my hubris? What a mess! I do believe that, in whatever way was available to me, I went looking for the truth about God. Yet I tend to think that when I'm investigating an issue, such as belief in God, I'm going to look at things for "just the facts." For instance, when I initially grappled with the question of Jesus's resurrection, I treated the whole endeavor as an academic research project. *Well, the facts suggest that either Jesus rose from the dead or he did not rise from the dead. Logically, both cannot be true. So I'm going to have to go with the hypothesis with the most explanatory power . . . wherever the data leads.*

I had such an idealistic view of my endeavor. Curiously, I

didn't carefully think through that it wasn't an abstract idea or impersonal hypothesis that I was investigating, but a person. At the end of my investigation, if I believed that God was real, I wasn't just faced with accepting a set of facts but a real person. Why does that matter? Because not only did I wonder whether belief in Jesus was merited, but I still had a lingering distrust of people, and Jesus is a person.

A friend of mine illustrates the relational side of doubt in his own work and life. Dr. Gary Habermas devoted his doctoral work at Michigan State University toward analyzing the evidence for the historical nature of Jesus's resurrection. He collected and read all the scholarly writing he could find concerning the resurrection, around 2,400 sources at that time.[11] In assimilating the material, Gary used only the facts that could be stated without belief in the Bible as inspired or reliable (this was in part due to the demands of his dissertation committee). He calls this method "the minimal facts argument." He discovered that there was a wealth of evidence pointing toward a resurrected Jesus two thousand years ago. Through debates, teaching, speaking, and writing, Gary has been defending his belief that the resurrection is historical ever since, around forty years.

Though Gary's life is full of speaking engagements and scholarly writing on the facts of the resurrection, he openly discusses, and even writes about, the doubt he experienced in suffering through his wife's stomach cancer and consequent death. Even though he was convinced through his own dissertation research that Jesus died and rose from the dead, when faced with such a great burden as the death of a loved one, the questions began to overwhelm him. Did the truth of the Christian faith have

---

11 Now up to 3,500 sources in his analysis.

anything to say when you're not dealing with just a set of facts but with a devastating emotional experience? Why would God allow such suffering for Debbie, Gary, and their family? What did he believe about Jesus in light of his wife's death?

As Gary struggled to even want to find the answers to his own questioning, he came to a game-changing realization. If God is real and he raised Jesus from the dead, then God *has demonstrated* that he is trustworthy and in control, even when Gary doesn't have "all the facts." He writes:

> He [God] created the world, raised His Son from the dead, made a path of salvation for us, answered our prayers, and prepared heaven for us. So why do we find it so difficult to trust Him in our present circumstances?[12]

Based on what he already knew about God, Gary could trust God even in the things he did not know. For him, though, it wasn't an easily won trust because the circumstances were so devastating, and God never answered him on why his family was suffering. Now, don't forget, Gary was already convinced of the truth of the resurrection of Jesus as an historical fact. But he still needed to apply that truth to his relationship with God.

After learning about Gary's experience, I felt as though I'd been hit smack in the noggin by the reality-check fairy. *What have I been doing? I've been investigating God as a set of facts without acknowledging my distrust of persons!* Even if I come to the propositional belief that God is real, I may not trust him. I wasn't acknowledging this aspect of the search for answers. I'd

---

12 Gary Habermas, *The Risen Jesus and Future Hope* (Lanham, MD: Rowman & Littlefield, 2003), 195.

learned to distrust persons, and God wasn't exempt. So, though I'd like to think that my search for answers could be all calculation and no counseling, it just wasn't true. In addition, over the years of discussing belief in God, I've only personally engaged with one person who changed his mind about God after accepting the intellectual arguments, only one "Mr. Spock" who felt he had to logically accept a different viewpoint when he recognized his own viewpoint was refuted.

I struggle with the atheist-versus-theist posturing. Both sides claim to be logical. Both sides say that their factual evidence leads to the logical conclusion . . . as if that's the only thing going on here. Yet what should I say of the reality of the situation? If God is real, God is not reducible to a set of empirical facts. If I choose to trust God, it is the kind of trust, or faith, I give to a person with whom I have a relationship. This is not the kind of trust I would give to a scientific hypothesis or to an abstract idea such as justice. There is no personal element in these things. However, the Christian view of God is that he has personhood. He is a person. Therefore, doubt and trust are appropriated to him in a similar way that I appropriate these things to people. To be an honest doubter, I must understand the object of my doubt. In this case, there is no object, but rather a subject: the person of God.

Imagine if I were to treat my husband's love as a set of empirically verifiable facts. "Roger, I want to know if you love me. Therefore, I'm going to collect a bunch of data and evidence. Then I will make a conclusion on whether to trust you based on my comparison of the data. If more evidences build up on the 'not loved' side of the balance than the 'loved' side, I must conclude that you do not love me. I will not take into consideration your thoughts, the difficulties of expressing yourself to another human being, that you may not have said everything you feel about me, that my perception could be wrong, or even that my desires might influence my interpretation of the data. Rather, my conclusion will be based solely on my observation of the data." What kind of conclusion might I discover? Who knows! But is this a fair way to assess my husband's love to see if I should put my trust in him? And what if Roger did set about to "prove" his love to me because of my conclusion? Would I not be considered an overly suspicious or mean-spirited person for putting him through such a test in order to show that he loves me after all he has already done for me? As C. S. Lewis writes, "No man is our friend who believes in our good intentions only when they are proved. . . . Confidence, between one man and another, is in fact almost universally praised as a moral beauty, not blamed as a logical error."[13]

So I've discovered one of the reasons I have trouble trusting God: he is a real person, and he can give me as little or as much knowledge of himself as he deems appropriate. A collection of plant cells under a microscope cannot make decisions about how to appropriate the knowledge of themselves, for the cells have no "selves." Most of the time, I completely ignore the fact that God has a will. I want to look at God under a microscope and find out everything about him as though he has no "self" and therefore no say in the matter. Yet as I stop to think about what I want from God, I realize that I am not even treating him with the respect I would give to one of my fellow humans.

You may ask, "With all this talk of trust, aren't you just advocating for an uncritical faith?" Am I really, though? Is it uncritical of me to desire to trust a person? This is what humans do: we

---

13 C. S. Lewis, *The World's Last Night: And Other Essays* (San Francisco: Harper-One, 2017), 25–26, Kindle.

trust, or not. I lean rather toward not trusting others because I tend to expect the worst. To trust God, a being whom I cannot physically see, smell, hear,[14] or touch, is a daily challenge. But it's not that there is a lack of evidence of his existence. There's plenty of evidence to investigate. Rather, the challenge is that it is inappropriate and ungenerous of me to give God the same treatment I give to impersonal things. I have been guilty of doing so. I have engaged in much theorizing about God rather than directly engaging in relationship with him. In fact, I had this **reductivist** attitude since the beginning of my doubt. I set out to discover a set of facts that would prove or disprove "belief" about God. My distrust in people had produced distrust in the person of God, a relational doubt. I used intellectual objections to buttress my aversion to a relationship with God.

Reductivist: The tendency to reduce to a minimum or to simplify in an extreme way.

Adapted from Wiktionary, s.v. "reductivist," https://en.wiktionary.org/wiki/reductivist.

So now I held two opposing hopes: (1) that I would find answers that would vindicate my belief in God while also demonstrating the wretched state of the church, or (2) that I would find answers so strongly against belief in God that I could begin the long walk away from faith and the church. I didn't know what I wanted except that I wanted freedom. I wanted freedom from the enslavement to faulty, human-designed culture and expectations. I wanted freedom from feeling like I was wearing someone else's belief clothes. I wanted my own wardrobe, one that felt

---

14 A student at a conference asked me if I've ever heard God's voice. I said, "Do you mean physically?" He replied, "Yes, physically." I answered, "I've never heard God speak audibly."

more natural to me. I longed for something I didn't know how to explain.

• CONSIDERATIONS •

1. Are you currently struggling with any doubt? Have you struggled in the past?
2. Do/did your doubts relate to any of the three mentioned above? Or do you have different doubts? What are they?
3. How do your emotions and desires affect your doubt?
4. What can you do to begin to answer those doubts?

CHAPTER 3

GOD, ARE YOU THERE?

The one who states his case first seems right,
until the other comes and examines him.

—PROVERBS 18:17

I can't roll my tongue. I am the only one in the family without
the ability to do so. Because of this, I am frequently the object of
teasing by ostentatious tongue rollers. I don't even know how the
teasing gets started. *Why do people view this ability as a talent?*
They suddenly start showing off as if they've put time and effort into
achieving the high goal of tongue rolling. As soon as the tongues
start rolling, it's quickly apparent that I am unlike the others. These
tongue rollers zero in on me and begin saying, "No, Mary Jo . . . it's
like this. You've just gotta roll the sides up. Watch me do it. Now you
try." I humor the tongue-rolling beings with a quick flex, creating
an indentation in my tongue. The laughter bursts out. *What is so
funny about this?* I haven't figured it out after all these years.

My church existence felt like being the one person in a room
who couldn't roll her tongue. I was the one person in Bible study

class who couldn't "just believe" in God, that is, without any kind of critical thinking on the matter. When I questioned a teaching, I would receive a *we're-better-than-you-because-we-can-roll-our-tongues* attitude, and a rather stuffy, awkward silence. It was the loud kind of silence that says, "You're not one of us and we don't appreciate your question." I'm not entirely positive that my feeling matched the reality of the situation, since as a minister's wife I may have been overly self-conscious about asking questions. However, I rarely had a person encourage my questioning or thoughtfully engage in answering a hard question, especially if they had to commit to more time beyond that class session. I began to interpret church as a holy tongue-rollers association. *Here at the church, our motto is: You've either got faith or you don't. We've got faith. We're better than you.*

Naturally, I concluded: *So this is the way it's going to be: if I want answers to difficult questions, the church is not here to help.* Therefore, I ventured outside the church, deciding to listen to debates between Christians and atheists. I figured that was a good plan, since I could get both sides of the arguments presented. Internet websites and blogging were still fairly young (Facebook wasn't even open to non-college students yet), but I managed to find a debate on God's existence that some atheists seemed to greatly value. And this debate between opposing viewpoints was important to me.

Too often I have found the church adamantly focused on only one viewpoint: their own. Perhaps that is one reason I felt so out of place in the church. My cultural background was so different from Southern evangelical culture that I think it was difficult for church people to understand me at even a superficial level. I value opposing viewpoints in part because I grew up with a viewpoint far different from the viewpoint of the churches we served. Yet I frequently heard church members use denigrating statements about people with differing viewpoints. It was infuriating.

Get out of your insular bubble, I would think. *Gain some experience with people who differ from you. Stop reacting out of desire-driven emotion. Yeah, you heard me: emotion. You are not representing God's Word nor truth. You are emoting. Hold yourself accountable for truth, actual truth, and not what is easiest to accept in order to get on with life.* Many car rides home from church were heated engagements on this very issue. Roger frequently cautioned that he thought I was being less than gracious in my treatment of the church. Of course, his comments would further anger me. *You don't understand. You're one of them.* I assumed I wouldn't get any help by asking him questions either (I mean . . . he *is* a tongue roller).

MY FIRST ENCOUNTER WITH
CHRISTIAN DEBATE

The first debate I found was between Christian philosopher William Lane Craig and atheist philosopher Austin Dacey at California State University. I managed to grab a downloadable audio file so that I could listen to it in my truck on the way to and from work. Before playing the audio file, I reflected on what was about to happen. I felt fairly certain that the atheist arguments would annihilate any faith that remained in my life. From the little I had seen, atheists were extremely confident in presenting their arguments. I hadn't read or listened to anyone who doubted their atheism in the way I doubted my theism. *What was I hoping to find? What did I really want to prove?* Not sure whether I was ready for what was to come, I pressed the play button.

After many instructions and welcoming statements, Christian philosopher William Lane Craig began his opening arguments. Craig, a very organized debater, clearly outlined six major points to argue for the existence of God: the contingency argument, the cosmological argument, the fine-tuning argument, the moral argument, the argument for the resurrection, and the argument from religious experience. I'd never heard of these arguments before, except the resurrection argument, which I had discovered in *The Case for Christ*. As I listened, I wondered, *Why, in a decade of church life, have I never been exposed to these arguments?* An odd mixture of refreshment upon hearing the arguments and discontent with my church education welled up within me as I listened. What's more, while the arguments sounded pretty good, I really didn't know much about making good arguments for God's existence. I told myself, *Wait for the atheist arguments. They are going to be challenging. You'll see; Christians have been hiding their ignorance behind authoritarianism and church culture.*

Dr. Austin Dacey moved to the podium, and I could hear the rustling of the audience as they began to shift to a new point of view. *Here we go.* Dacey also offered an organized presentation, outlining five arguments against the existence of God: the hiddenness of God, the success of science in explaining nature without the need for supernatural agency, the dependence of the mind on physical processes in the brain, naturalistic evolution, and pointless evil and suffering. He was a calm, cool, collected academic, and I was expecting him to do some serious shredding of the Christian belief in God. Yet, as his arguments unfurled, I began to wonder how much Dacey had studied Christianity. While he didn't make overtly bad arguments, it seemed he lacked a robust understanding of the Christian beliefs he was criticizing. At this point, I was not trained in Christian theology, other than sneaking peeks at my husband's seminary books. And I hadn't been trained at all in philosophy. However, there were some obvious problems (and I'll use some of the terms I later learned to describe these issues later in the book).

Dacey argued that if there is a God, we would expect that he would ensure that everyone believes in him, at least everyone who can reciprocate a love relationship. One should expect to find clear evidence of God's existence, such as a booming voice heard all over the earth saying, "I am that I am." What we find instead is that there is no evidence that would persuade all reasonable people.

I found a point to pause the audio file and thought on this statement for a moment. *Wait a minute, doesn't Christianity teach that God has empirically revealed himself over and over and yet people still rejected him?* God used a loud voice in Deuteronomy 4:12–13 and 5:23–25, and the people responded negatively. Elijah called fire down from heaven, and some people still rejected God (1 Kings 18–19). Jesus performed miracles in front of the masses, and yet many walked away not believing in him. He even resurrected people from the dead, and people still didn't believe in who he was or what he said. There's something else going on here. Humans don't always "believe it when they see it."

For instance, President Dwight D. Eisenhower knew this tendency of people to discount what they don't want to believe. So he was especially careful to document his concentration camp visits during the Second World War. In an April 1945 letter to General George C. Marshall, he wrote this about his visit to a concentration camp in Germany: "The things I saw beggar description. . . . The visual evidence and the verbal testimony of starvation, cruelty and bestiality were so overpowering as to leave me a bit sick. . . . I made the visit deliberately, in order to be in position to give first-hand evidence of these things if ever, in the future, there develops a tendency to charge these allegations merely to 'propaganda.'"[1] He later

---

1   Letter, DDE to George C. Marshall, 15 April 1945, from *The Papers of Dwight David Eisenhower, The War Years IV*, doc #2418, www.dwightdeisenhower.com/187/Holocaust-Concentration-Camps.

wrote in his memoir *Crusade in Europe*, "I felt that the evidence should be immediately placed before the American and British publics in a fashion that would leave no room for cynical doubt."

Eisenhower ordered the collection of documentation of the Holocaust, resulting in 80,000 feet of film footage, which was used as evidence in the Nuremberg trials.[2] Eisenhower also collected numerous photos, including ones of himself at concentration camps to provide evidence of his firsthand witness. Yet it didn't take long for Holocaust deniers to appear. These deniers are people who have access to an abundance of testimony and evidence of the existence of the Holocaust. Somehow, with all the evidence available, the Holocaust deniers remain unconvinced of this horrific event in human history. How is it possible with so much evidence to remain unconvinced, to believe it's all false? Ultimately, I don't know, since I cannot reach inside the mind of any given individual. However, I'm inclined to think that other factors, such as desires, emotion, and agendas, play a significant role in what humans believe. While Holocaust deniers may be an extreme example, their existence demonstrates that even in the presence of much evidence, human beings are quite capable of disbelief.

Yet, even still, wouldn't it be better if God just announced himself to the world? My thoughts were interrupted by my arrival at work. Though I had a busy day of teaching ahead, I couldn't get my mind off this point.

By the end of the school day, as usual, I was physically and emotionally spent. Keeping up with teens, even as a thirty-year-old, was quite taxing. However, I was anxious to get back to the

---

2   Lawrence Douglas, "Film as Witness: Screening Nazi Concentration Camps before the Nuremberg Tribunal," *The Yale Law Journal* 105.2 (November 1995): 449–81, www.jstor.org/stable/797126.

debate. I got into my blue 1999 Toyota Tacoma, started up the engine, and immediately began listening to the debate again.

The Christian debater, Craig, offered a rebuttal to Dacey's point about the hiddenness of God. "So whether God gives a booming testimony or writes in the sky, it doesn't necessarily guarantee that people will come into relationship with him; it might even have the opposite effect."

The opposite effect. Why hadn't I thought of that? I know that *I'm* prone to a rebellious streak, even when I'm trying to look as though my arguments are completely dispassionate and sterile. God's voice might not make me submit to him or love him, but instead, resent him. I might think: *Why can't he just be more gentle? Humans can be gentle and subtle in how they develop relationships. What's the matter with God? Why does he have to be such a cosmic bully?*

Dacey is not the only one to criticize the hiddenness of God. The great science popularizer Carl Sagan once posited that if God exists, he should just place a glowing cross of stars in the sky so we can all be sure of him. It's the same line of reasoning, and I'm discovering it has the same response: *because, humans.* We are such a complex bunch of creatures. Just like Holocaust deniers, some humans would deny that the cross was a sign of God. Other humans may attempt to worship just the starry cross. There would be a wide range of responses to the "show and tell" situation if God were to present himself in these ways. It's not as simple as, "Hey, Perfect Being, show yourself and we'll all be good to go."

Since God's goal, in accordance with Christianity, is to draw people into a loving relationship with himself, Craig argued that he didn't see how a further demonstration of God's existence over the evidence already given would accomplish that goal.

In return, Dacey responded that a clear revelation of God needs to be more effective in proving God exists and in drawing more people in to a saving love relationship with him. If God remains hidden, then the probability of people coming into a loving relationship with him is zero.

With this assertion, Dacey's particular atheistic line of argumentation disappointed me. He seemed to have missed the bigger idea of free will. Of course, God wants people to come into a loving relationship with him, but not at the cost of their free will. Where does Dacey draw the line with how far God could reveal himself and yet still allow for people to freely choose him rather than their belief be the result of an unavoidable consequence?[3] Should human autonomy not matter to the Creator? Dacey seemed to argue for a cosmic bully who doesn't care about us, other than that we know he's large and in charge. However, the Christian God is not a cosmic bully. It makes sense for him to keep a distance in order to not overwhelm our free will with a coercive presence. If forced or coerced, we would not be in a truly loving relationship but in a dystopian embrace of a dictatorial superior. Dacey seemed to miss out on some of the important considerations of theology, which was unexpected and startling to me.

A UNIVERSE OUT OF NOTHING

The debate waged on. Craig systematically responded to each of Dacey's points, but in rebuttals, Dacey began to resort to the "we don't know" type of answer. For example, Dacey challenged Craig's view of the origin of the universe as *creation ex nihilo*

---

3 An "unavoidable consequence" that only perhaps an illness or mental disease could possibly keep you from rejecting (such as a disease that alters reality or gives one hallucinations).

on the basis that it was a new kind of causal effect for which we have no other forms to explore for verification. Yet, on his own view of the universe, he would still have the same problem, just in another form. As Craig pointed out, *creation ex nihilo* lacks a physical cause but has a productive cause in the person of God. In atheism, the universe lacks not only a physical cause but also a productive cause. The universe would literally be considered as coming from nothing, though the verification for something coming from nothing is itself nonexistent.

Creation ex nihilo: The belief that God created the universe out of nothing; the Latin term *ex nihilo* means "out of nothing."

Dacey's response to the problem was akin to "we just don't know" and "it's premature to speculate on the matter." I actually somewhat agree with his position in that we do not know the answer in full. However, he also did not acknowledge what can be deduced from what we do know. Craig argued from deductive reasoning that universes need causes because they have a beginning. Something had to cause the universe to begin . . . and something is not the same as nothing.

I thought on the matter for a bit while sitting in the driveway at home. Then I remembered a lecture in my undergraduate geology class on the various elements present in the early stages of the universe. The professor set up his lecture with these words: "When the universe created itself . . ."

Hold on . . . what? Did he just say that the universe made itself? The universe caused itself to come into existence without any previously existing physical or productive cause? What does that even mean?

The professor stated these words in passing as if this wildly speculative theory was a solid fact that everyone knows. It felt like he was saying some nonsense akin to "when the fire melted, causing the unicorns to freeze . . ." That moment in class, his words hit me like an unexpected punch line from a stand-up comedy routine, and I laughed out loud. I was amazed that the professor nonchalantly said something so ludicrous. He didn't even try to offer a caveat by suggesting alternative theories!

While I'm a Christian, my atheist background nudges me with reminders of things I used to think about the weirdness of the Christian faith. So I sympathize with those who find Christian beliefs difficult to understand or believe. On occasion, I've found myself during a sermon thinking, *Yes, but how do you know that? You've not explained any reason for us to think that is true. You expect us to accept it without reasoning.* However, I suppose I was using a double standard by not expecting to find any weirdness in atheist beliefs, like those of my undergraduate geology professor.

Now, even after listening to Dacey give atheist arguments at such a high level of thought, I wasn't satisfied. The further Dacey dove into his arguments, the more dissatisfied I became with his understanding of Christian beliefs, as well as his understanding of the challenges to atheism. At the time, I was hoping the case against Christian theism would be stronger, possibly crushing. But this was only one debate. In two hours, these two gentlemen couldn't sum up the whole debate on theism versus atheism. There was so much more I needed to understand.

AN UNPLANNED DEGREE

I gathered up my things from the truck and went to the mailbox, where I pulled out a copy of the *Christian Research Journal*. I had recently subscribed to the journal to find answers to my theological questions. However, my mind had now shifted to dinner plans. Roger and Emily would be home soon. So I placed the journal, along with my work bag, in our bedroom and went to the kitchen to begin dinner.

Roger and Emily soon arrived and began to help. We all chatted about our day. Emily discussed her teachers and what she was learning, while Roger discussed challenges at the church. Usually I chimed in with stories from my day. I taught middle and high school band and enjoyed how unpredictable the kids could be at times . . . and yet still so predictable. But today I was uncharacteristically quiet. Not only were my thoughts consumed by the debate I had just listened to, I was also embroiled in a search for a master's degree in music education—a search that wasn't going too well. Most of the schools nearby were too expensive, and the ones that were affordable I didn't like. Meanwhile, the schools where I did want to study weren't showing much interest in me. I was a bit distraught. Ever since my sophomore year in high school, I'd planned out my education in music. I knew exactly when I was going to get a master's degree and knew that I wanted to move into teaching at the university level. It was time to take the next step, but the opportunities weren't presenting themselves.

After dinner, I went into our bedroom and sat in the office chair in the reading nook. While thinking about grad school, I picked up my new journal and began to flip through it to get a feel for the articles inside. Suddenly, something caught my eye. I stared down at an advertisement for a master's degree at a university unknown to me.[4] "Earn a master's degree in apologetics . . . Study with Gary Habermas, William Lane Craig, J. P. Moreland, and more . . ."

This is it! This is the degree I'm going to pursue.

---

4 Biola University.

I couldn't believe my own thoughts, so I began to argue with myself:

"What are you saying to yourself? You don't know anything about this university or this degree!"

> I don't care. I know that I'm going to get an apologetics degree. This program is the answer to my problem.

"No, it is not the answer. You are a music educator. You've planned your life for years. Sure, you've made a few errors in judgment along the way, but you're still basically on track. This slick advertisement is just messing with you at a vulnerable moment."

> Is it? I don't think so. I've been focused on finding answers. Here's a way to find some answers.

"We're poor! It's frivolous to spend money on something that won't advance my career. Besides, Roger doesn't even know that I've been studying apologetics. I can't waste time on a degree that has nothing to do with my current career."

> Would you like to keep trying more excuses? Or are you willing to take a risk to see if what you believe is true? You've forgotten yourself. You are a risk taker . . . or at least a cautious risk taker.

I sat in the chair, staring at the advertisement, suspended in thought. My mind raced through the possible consequences of such an academic pursuit. For that moment, I felt frozen in time, as though I was facing a door to a different universe and pondering if I should walk through it.

At that moment, Roger came into the room. I looked at him with an expression full of intent, and he quickly saw that something was up.

"What is it, JoJo?"

"I've figured out my master's degree."

"Oh, okay. What did you figure out?"

"I'm going here to do this degree." I got up, walked over to him, and placed the journal in his hands.

He read the advertisement and said, "What is *apologetics*?"

"It's what I've been studying on my own."

"I don't know what that is."

"It's a branch of theology dedicated to answering objections to Christian beliefs, as well as to building a positive case for belief in Christianity. I've been having a difficult time with my faith in God. I have so many questions about him and about this life that the church isn't really trying to answer. I've had troubles believing all this is true, especially with how bad my experience in church has been so far. I think you've noticed. I've been extra cranky and impatient with you and Emily. But now I know what I need to do. I need to do this degree, because it's about finding those answers."

"But I thought you were dead set on getting your music education master's degree. You wanted to teach at the university. What are you going to do with this degree? What job does it lead to?"

"I don't know."

Roger paused and looked back at the advertisement. He didn't look frustrated. He was probably initially "working the numbers" while trying to process this complete turn-about on my plans. One of the ways that Roger has always been supportive of me is by figuring out how to do practically what I imagine theoretically. He's the grounding source for my high-flying dreams and ideas.

Finally, he looked up at me. "Okay, well, let's check it out. You just caught me off guard. You were so adamant about your music degree that I didn't see this one coming."

I smiled. "Yeah, neither did I."

As Roger left the room to go do some research on the university and on the word *apologetics*, I felt a slight twinge of fear. I wasn't expecting him to be so supportive right off the bat. I thought he'd put up a fight or tell me I was crazy. At the very least, I thought he'd say we didn't have the money to fund such an endeavor. On the contrary, he was already off and running to try to bring some reality to my outrageous idea. I was potentially going to go through with this nonsensical use of my time and resources. *Panic!* My mind raced with rationalizations of how I did not have time to do this degree. I felt foolish yet excited, and ready to go but apprehensive. In my whole life, I'd never made such a dramatic decision in such a short amount of time.

This doesn't make sense, right? Right. So I applied to the university, got accepted, and began studies that fall.

• CONSIDERATIONS •

1. Which, if any, of the arguments for God's existence impress you? Why? If none do, why not?
2. How have experiences in the church affected your view of God?
3. Do you ever hope to discover there is no God?
4. How far would you be willing to go to discover whether your beliefs are true?

CHAPTER 4

RESURRECTION

The man who agrees with us that some question, little regarded by others, is of great importance, can be our Friend. He need not agree with us about the answer.

—C. S. LEWIS, *THE FOUR LOVES*

"You talked with who, about what?" I stood in the family room, looking with disbelief at my husband.

"My friend, Deanna, at seminary. She serves on a leadership team, and they are looking for an apologist to speak at the state evangelism conference."

A slight dread at the direction this conversation was going caused me to add a bit of sarcasm to my response. "And so you recommended some well-known and experienced speaker, right?"

Roger smiled sheepishly. "No, I said, 'I know an apologist. I'm married to her.'"

"What! I'm not an 'apologist!' I'm a first-semester student in an apologetics degree. What were you thinking?" I had just started my studies and barely knew the names of my professors, much less a presentable theological argument for God's existence.

"I was thinking you are perfect for the job. Anyway, Deanna will be calling you soon to discuss the details."

"But, honey . . . I'm not ready for that. I don't even know what I would speak on. I mean, I appreciate your enthusiasm, but really. I need more time *and* education. I'm not a public speaker. And I'm not an apologist!"

"Well, you're in an apologetics degree, you're a good speaker at your band concerts, and you're also a woman. They are looking for a woman to speak on apologetics. I think it's a match."

I rolled my eyes. "Well, I don't like it, but I'll talk with her before I make a final decision."

One short phone call later, I was committed to speaking at the Oklahoma State Evangelism Conference. I was worried. What did I really know about anything? *Nothing. You don't really know anything.* I had actually tried to convince Roger's friend that she would be better off trying to get the author and public speaker Lee Strobel. With the gracious demeanor of a bull in a china shop, I asked, "What's the matter, wasn't Strobel available?" Deanna was unflinching in her pursuit. She was certain that I was the one to speak at the event. When I discovered that I'd only have to do a breakout session, I was much more amenable to the idea.

However, I still had no idea what topic I should present at this event. The only guidance given was that I needed to speak "on apologetics." I needed help, but up to this point I had been doing this whole apologetics thing alone. The only people I felt I could reach out to for help were my instructors at the university, whom I didn't know well and had never met personally. I emailed the program director, who told me to give Professor Clay Jones a call.

MY FIRST SPEAKING GIG

So I phoned Dr. Jones, introduced myself, and explained my dilemma. "I'm in trouble," I told him. "I've committed to a presentation on apologetics at a statewide event, and I have no idea what I'm doing."

"Wow! Well, praise God that you have such an opportunity."

The genuine excitement in my professor's voice actually made me more nervous. I secretly hoped he was going to tell me that I couldn't do this because I didn't have enough experience.

"Oh, no, I really tried to convince the organizers that I'm not fit to do such a thing, since I have no experience. But they were quite convinced."

"I think it's great. Let's talk about what you're going to present. What's your subject?"

"That's just it. I don't have a subject. The organizers just said, 'apologetics.'"

"Ahhh. I see. In that case, you should do the resurrection. The resurrection is foundational in the Christian faith. If Christ wasn't raised, the apostle Paul says our faith is useless. That's quite a statement! When you read Acts, the resurrection is what the apostles were constantly going back to, saying this is the evidence. Acts 17 is Paul discussing the proof of who Jesus is by giving evidence to all men in raising him from the dead and so on. I mean, you don't have to do resurrection, but I think a lot of apologists today are making a mistake by not spending enough time on the resurrection. The power of the gospel is in the fact that Jesus really did die on the cross and that Jesus really was raised from the dead. That's where I would start."

"The evidence of the resurrection was one of the arguments

that I found compelling in my own struggle with faith," I said. "I'm a bit familiar with the arguments. How would you proceed?"

"Well, what we need to do is develop the major evidences for the resurrection, and those to me are fairly straightforward.

"First, there is historical evidence that Jesus died of crucifixion. John Dominic Crossan, the cofounder of the Jesus Seminar, and Gert Lüdemann, the atheist German theologian, both agree that Jesus Christ was crucified. That Jesus Christ was crucified is about as clear as anything historical can ever be.

"Second, the tomb was found empty. I would make the case for that. If the tomb wasn't empty, of course then, wow, I don't know what everyone is doing because they could have stopped; they could have ended Christianity right there. All they had to do was produce the body. So that's a hard one for the skeptic to get around.

"And after that, the disciples began to proclaim that they had seen the risen Jesus, and so I'd make the point that the disciples began to proclaim that they saw Jesus raised from the dead.

"Finally, I think I'd point out that they were doing this in the face of great danger and often it resulted in persecution and even death. I mean, we know extrabiblically that James the brother of Jesus was stoned to death by the Sanhedrin. Why? We like to ask the question, why? How much evidence would it take for you to so believe that your brother was God that you would die for him? We also have a lot of extra biblical evidence that Paul was beheaded by Nero. Why did Paul give his life if indeed Jesus wasn't raised from the dead? And so that's always basically been my approach."

"Okay, I'm taking so many notes that I think my hand is starting to smoke."

I finished up the conversation with Dr. Jones, thanked him,

and let him know I'd report back in after the presentation to let him know how it went. He was definitely more excited for me than I was.

As January rapidly approached, I began to feel uncomfortable that I was speaking on apologetics without first dealing with two things: (1) coming to terms with church ministry, and (2) sharing my faith with my own extended family. *How can I talk to all these people about belief in God when I've harbored such ill feelings toward the church? And how can I give a presentation to strangers when I haven't even really talked with my family about what I've learned?* I had already determined that my issues with the church had no easy solution. I accepted the tension in that situation.

The second concern made me feel a bit disingenuous. My family was getting together in Portland for Christmas, as usual. Roger and I had discussed God in small doses with various family members at various times, but I didn't feel it was enough. If I was going to study apologetics and speak publicly about God, I needed my family to understand why I was taking this path. I struggled to come up with the best way to introduce the whole family to apologetics. Finally, I hit upon a solution. *That's it! I'll buy everyone a book!* So for Christmas that year, every member of my family received a copy of Strobel's *The Case for Christ* in their stocking.

Of course, this method demonstrated a bit of cowardice on my part. But it fit the cultural expectations of my family. Northwesterners don't shove religious talk in people's faces, but I figured a book wasn't too pushy. Ultimately, the gift received various reactions, from the inquisitive to the dismissive. But I did my part. I could now move on to my commitment and give that first talk on apologetics.

The presentation came and all went well. Being a bit

obsessive-compulsive, I had overprepared for the presentation, but as a result I was able to thoughtfully engage all the questions at the end. My fears, as usual, ended up being unfounded. The leader of the event even put me on the main stage to discuss the importance of apologetics. So, with my first presentation under my belt, I entered a new semester in my degree program.

I took a course called "In Defense of the Resurrection" with Dr. Clay Jones and Dr. Gary Habermas. I assumed the course was to teach us reasons for believing in the **historicity** of the resurrection. What I didn't expect was that we would be tasked with arguing a case for the resurrection with a person who didn't believe it to be true. Our assignment had two options: (1) start a blog defending the resurrection, or (2) have an email conversation defending the

Historicity: Having actually occurred in history as opposed to being a legend or myth; the historical actuality of a claim or event.

resurrection. I wasn't excited about this assignment at all. It was one thing to speak to a group of people who believed like I did, but it was a whole other thing to try to convince someone who disagreed with me. In fact, my stomach took a few turns as I read the instructions.

Wow, there's no way I'm going near that first option. It's way too public. People will think I'm some kind of religious nut job. And that second option . . . yuck. Why can't we just write a paper on this? Jeez, professor. I would've tried to argue with the professor for a more private or friendly option if I didn't have my kind of pride. I was proud of my academic skill and wanted professors and fellow students to think well of me. As a result, I was going to do that assignment and do it well, even if it meant going against my cultural upbringing.

Who was I going to ask to do this challenge with me? I didn't know many people outside my immediate spheres of public school music and church. Was it even appropriate to ask a work colleague to argue with me on religion? Couldn't I lose my job for that?

One day I sat in my office at school worrying over this wretched assignment. Just then my flute instructor walked in to begin her day of teaching private lessons. She was a red-headed, assertive, snarky, but genuinely gracious woman who was highly accomplished on her instrument. She was also a no-nonsense kind of person who valued her intelligence greatly. Plus, I knew she didn't attend church. Part of me thought that she'd be great to ask, and the other part of me thought that I'd lose my flute instructor if I did ask. Before my overanalysis led to paralysis, I decided to dive off the cliff and just ask.

"Good morning, Mara. Hey, I need help with a project for my graduate degree."

Taken a bit off guard, she replied, "Oh yeah? What are you getting a degree in?"

Almost apologetically, I explained, "It's a degree in apologetics, which means I'm learning how to make a case for what I believe about God."

"Sounds interesting," she said with a hint of caution.

"Yes, it's quite fascinating. I have an assignment in which I need to have a discussion with a person who doesn't believe that Jesus rose from the dead. My job is to make the case that he did rise from the dead. If I've guessed correctly, you'd actually be great for this project."

"Hmm. Well, what would I have to do?"

"You'd have to be willing to email back and forth with me a few times on the issue."

To my surprise, Mara showed a glimmer of excitement. "I think this will be great," she said. "My husband is a philosophy professor at the university. He's also an atheist. I'm going to get him in on the fun."

"Oh, um, thanks. Yes, it'll be great."

Oh, man. What am I getting myself into? How in the blazes did I choose the one person I know who just happens to be married to an atheist philosophy professor? Sometimes my life feels like an amateurishly written movie script.

At first, I wanted to curse Dr. Jones and his crazy assignment. But then I realized I probably needed to do this exchange. So far in my Christian life, I had not had to substantiate my beliefs in any truly meaningful way. I'd been assuming Christianity was true or assuming it was not true; I'd never worked through my beliefs in a situation in which people adamantly disagreed with me. I decided, *Dr. Jones may be a devilishly crafty genius, or he may be an ingeniously crafty devil.*

THE EXCHANGE

I wrote the first email to Mara, my writing laced with the self-serving desire to show that I was an intelligent, thoughtful, studied human being. The letter began with all the warmth of a dispassionate lawyer's opening argument in a court of law:

> In the course of this email, I am going to lay down a foundation for the historicity of the resurrection of Jesus Christ. Please note that due to the brevity of the email, not all documentation will be given to you, but upon request, I can send it along.
>
> Historians of various persuasions and biblical scholars

from liberal to conservative tend to differ on the amount of historical content that can be found in the New Testament. However, nearly all these scholars who have

Textual criticism: The process of attempting to figure out the original wording of a text; reconstruction of the original manuscript.

studied the texts agree upon *certain* facts as being established historically. (Here an assumption is made that you accept **textual criticism** as a part of the process for establishing historical events and people.) I am mainly concerned with the events surrounding the end of Jesus's life. Those facts are:

1. Jesus died by Roman crucifixion.
2. He was buried, most likely in a private tomb.
3. Soon afterward, the disciples were discouraged, bereaved, and despondent, having lost hope.
4. Jesus's tomb was found empty very soon after his interment.*
5. The disciples had experiences that they believed were actual appearances of the risen Jesus.
6. Due to these experiences, the disciples' lives were thoroughly transformed, even being willing to die for this belief.
7. The proclamation of the resurrection took place very early, at the beginning of church history.
8. The disciples' public testimony and preaching of the resurrection took place in the city of Jerusalem, where Jesus had been crucified and buried shortly before.
9. The gospel message centered on the death and resurrection of Jesus.

10. Sunday was the primary day for gathering and worshiping.
11. James, the brother of Jesus and a former skeptic, was converted when, he believed, he saw the risen Jesus.
12. Just a few years later, Saul of Tarsus (Paul) became a Christian believer due to an experience that he believed was an appearance of the risen Jesus.

I find facts numbers 1, 4, 5, 6, 8, 11, and 12 of particular interest. If historians can establish these facts as being reliable through textual criticism, then we have a dilemma on our hands. Who was this person (and who did he claim to be)? How did he come back from the dead? Why did these people die for their belief in him? If we don't accept this history, what other history do we have to ignore as well? What are the implications to us if we consider these facts to be established?

I hope to answer some of these questions and more for you as we discuss these matters.

Thanks,

Mary Jo

P.S. Some of the scholars referred to include Robert Funk, Geza Vermes, E. P. Sanders, Norman Perrin, Jürgen Moltmann, Gavin D'Costa, Luke Timothy Johnson, and Thorwald Lorenzen.

* This fact is not as widely accepted as the rest, but a vast majority agree to it. Major source cited: *The Risen Jesus and Future Hope* by Gary Habermas. Rowman and Littlefield, 2003.

I read back over the email. I was initially pleased with myself and my academic tone. But I knew the moment I pushed the "send" button, I would second-guess myself and spend the rest of the night anticipating her response. After a second, third, and fourth reading, I finally sent it on to Mara.

I waited and waited for her reply. Her response came over an anxious week later:

Hi, Mary Jo,

I wasn't sure if you needed me to respond to this email or not, since you're just laying out your future arguments. Nonetheless, several thoughts came to mind while I was reading—things to consider when you send future email:

I will need as complete detail as possible when you send your arguments, including references to supporting documents. I am not a biblical scholar, and am interested in the supporting evidentiary writings upon which you are basing your theories.

Regarding the points you initially raise, I had thoughts about a few of them:

1. The four Gospels differ in their descriptions of the crucifixion. Take the case of the two robbers crucified alongside Jesus, for example. Three of the four Gospels mention the thieves, but one (John) leaves them out entirely, and of the other three accounts, two (Matthew and Mark) say that the thieves hurled abuse at Jesus as did the guards, but one (Luke) tells the famous story of the thief who repents upon the cross and rebukes the others. If Jesus's disciples were indeed witnesses to the crucifixion, arguably the most important event of their lives to date, and were inspired by it to write the Gospels, why would they give accounts that differ this dramatically? Since they do differ, how are we to decide what, if anything, is true?

2. (Response to point 5) It could be that Jesus didn't really die on the cross. There are many historical accounts of people who were thought to be dead and who were buried, but were actually buried alive—as evidenced by scratch marks from the insides of coffins that have been dug up, etc.

That the disciples believed they were in the actual presence of the risen Jesus does not mean that they really were. People believe all kinds of things that are not really true. People see Mary in a potato chip and believe she's really there. Millions of Catholics think that the pope can speak directly to God and is infallible. *Infallible*—even though there is no clear basis for this belief, and evidence to the contrary. Human conviction alone is not evidence of anything.

3. (Response to 6) That people are willing to die for a belief does not mean that the belief is true. Case in point—9/11 suicide bombers. There are so many examples that I could cite—I would hardly know where to begin. History is littered with the bodies of people who have died for false causes.

I won't be able to respond in any more meaningful way to your other points until I receive more information from you.

Mara

Mara had given me responses that I anticipated and in fact were some of the objections we'd been studying in the course. I smiled while quickly digging up all my studies on her objections. My anxiety had melted under the heat of my desire to argue well. In my second email, which was four single-spaced pages, or 2,800 words, I dove into the project of crushing her objections with the weight of as much evidence as I could currently muster. I meticulously referenced my points in footnotes, researching weblinks to go along with anything I had used from books that she couldn't access.

With her first question, I sought to denounce the idea that corroboration would imply collusion. If the Gospel accounts did indeed exactly match, we would have a case of four authors coming together to create a single story, or all borrowing their stories from the same source: a conspiracy of sorts. Rather, we had four stories with variants that all had the same core parts, the same basic story. This scenario was exactly what investigators of a crime hope to find: multiple, independent attestations that aren't just exact copies of each other. Noncorroborating testimonies about the same incident help investigators get past the subjectivity of individual human reports to the actual events that transpired.

I then gave a nonbiblical example of ancient textual reports of the Essene movement. Though four ancient authors reported on the Essenes, some of their details did not match up. Yet we don't throw out the Essenes as a real movement because there are differences in the reports. Rather, just like crime-scene investigators, we piece together the truth from those reports.

I skipped her second point, that Jesus could have been buried alive, and mentioned extra-biblical sources that attest to Jesus's death—the Roman historian Tacitus, the Jewish historian Josephus, Lucian of Samosata, Justin Martyr's dialog with Trypho. I explained the importance of the early nature of the testimony to Jesus's death and resurrection that Paul "passes on" in 1 Corinthians 15:3–5. The scholars place this testimony within two to three years after Jesus's death, which is much too early for legend to develop.[1]

After a lengthy footnoted section, I responded with some

---

1   The timeline establishing the early nature of the testimony in the creed in 1 Corinthians 15 may be found in Gary Habermas and Michael Licona, *The Case for the Resurrection of Jesus* (Grand Rapids: Kregel, 2004), 260.

quotes on the practice of Roman crucifixion from the *Journal of the American Medical Association* in an article entitled "On the Physical Death of Jesus Christ."[2] The Romans were masters of death by crucifixion. They had figured out one of the worst ways to inflict death. Crucifixion was considered unsurvivable. Even if we find an exception in history, we must remember that prior to his crucifixion, Jesus was scourged with a cat-of-nine-tails that ripped open his flesh and inflicted deep, severe wounds. It was harder for me to believe he could survive this brutal treatment than that he died, if we were to go by the evidence we had rather than speculate on possibilities.

My response was getting long. For her last two points, I agreed that human conviction alone is not much evidence, but once we place these believers in their culture, with the historical reliability of the Scriptures, add in archaeological evidence, the trustworthiness of their testimony, and the writings from non-Christian sources, we have a case worthy of serious investigation. I further agreed that people have died for a lie. However, there's a difference between dying for what you thought was true from secondhand information (for instance, the followers of Jim Jones, Muhammad, Buddha) and dying for what you experienced and knew firsthand was true, as with the earliest followers of Jesus. These were exponentially different scenarios, and I said I was unconvinced these disciples would have willingly suffered for decades until their horrible deaths for something they knew first-hand was false, just to keep perpetuating a lie with no reward of

2   William D. Edwards, Wesley J. Gabel, and Floyd E. Hosmer, "On the Physical Death of Jesus Christ," *Journal of American Medical Association* 255.11 (March 21, 1986): 1455–63, https://jamanetwork.com/journals/jama/article-abstract/403315.

fame, money, or power. Such a view seemed quite unreasonable. Something else must have happened.

Once finished, I again began to question everything I had written. I reread the email at least three times. *What have I left out? From where could she attack? What are the loopholes I left open to walk through?* I sat at my computer wondering what my move would be if I were arguing from atheism. It did not occur to me that this was a conversation, not a game of chess. Finally, I sent the email and waited for her next move.

I did not have to wait long this time for Mara to respond. She returned an email within a few days. Her email opened with: "Hi, Mary Jo. Okay, now we have more to go on." Mara responded in kind with over four pages of her own, at 3,000 words. She also made numerous references and linked to articles for me to review. Further, she gave up no ground, but rather dug in deeper into her objections. She ended with a zinger of a statement:

> What I've never understood, though, is why Christians are perfectly willing to admit that belief in their religion hinges on a "leap of faith," but are then constantly trying to offer "objective" evidence to support it. I think this is a mistake. If Christians simply relied on their faith as being rooted in spiritual beliefs of the supernatural, beliefs that would not and could not be held to scientific scrutiny, then they would be home free.

I was shocked. I knew from her interaction with my material that she'd been reading my evidences and arguments. From where was she getting this idea that I was promoting a "leap of faith"? I mentioned nothing like a leap of faith in my response. Rather, I usually shied away from the mysterious in Christianity due to my own naturalistic upbringing. Perhaps she was conflating my arguments with other experiences in her life. I hadn't considered how a person's experiences would color their view, including the way they engaged arguments. I thought I was trying to be the objective, white-coated lab scientist looking at the arguments without rose-colored glasses "tainting" or interpreting the facts. However, Mara had brought into our argument something we weren't even discussing, making me wonder about her previous experiences with church and/or Christians. Instead of pursuing that line of thought, however, I rushed rather hastily into responding.

My eagerness to prove my argument resulted in 5,400 words, and fifteen single-spaced pages of refutation. Her unusual twist at the end of her last response convinced me to ask her many more questions in this round. However, my questions were not those of a genuinely interested friend. Rather, I was leading the witness in my own kangaroo court.

- To say that "multiple attestation" is not acceptable is to disdain the standards applied by the scholars who do this work. And you are free to do so. But then who holds your criteria of allowable history in check?
- Are we not able to read the texts, cross-reference the early texts for consistency/inconsistency, and glean from them the information that is historically reliable no matter who is writing? We are going to put a lot of historians and textual scholars out of work here.
- All writers are coming from a bias. Does that mean we cannot trust any written information—newspapers, magazines, historical documents, the Constitution—to have objective truths of any kind?

- What parts of Jesus's death, empty tomb, and resurrection do not match? You have mentioned details surrounding the event, but not the event itself. How do we know what to glean when various reports appear contradictory?

And I couldn't allow that "leap of faith" statement to go unchecked. It seemed aimed at deriding a Christian's intelligence. My pride flared up, and I wasn't about to let someone tell me that my beliefs were ridiculous. I ended with this rebuttal:

> I did not personally come to Christ through a "leap of faith." This sounds like church lingo that I wouldn't have known, not being raised in church. I read the Bible all the way through, on my own, no churchgoing involved. A friend gave the Bible to me as a graduation gift. It was through my reasoning of what I read that I accepted it to be true.[3] Later on, I decided to see if Christianity's claims could withstand the arguments from atheists. That is why I am doing this now. The testing of something you believe to be true is always a good practice whether it be faith or no faith.

Ahhhh . . . yes, now I can hear the indignation in my own writing. My clear disdain for an anti-intellectual view of Christians came shining through, but it was clearly more about disliking being included in that statement. Self-preserving pride, as is so often the case, welled up in me and took command of this opportunity to witness, evangelize, or even to make good

---

3   I left out that I was invited to a church where I was moved to accept Christ after I had read the Bible.

conversation. My concern for Mara, as a person, if it was even present at all, was second to my concern for my own ability to argue well.

Mara gave up the conversation after receiving the fifteen-page academic paper that really should have been titled, "Why I'm Right and You are Wrong: Lessons in Self-Righteous Posturing with References and Footnotes." She thanked me for the engagement, but no longer had the time to go through all the material. I, however, felt that the conversation was a huge success and proudly sent it on to my professor, who gave me top marks.

Somehow, though, amid my self-aggrandizement was a sneaking sense of something like cowardice or fear. Why had I reacted so negatively to this assignment, especially the option of starting a blog to defend the resurrection? What was I afraid of? Yes, publicly speaking up about one's religious beliefs went against my cultural upbringing, but I felt a genuine sense of alarm that went beyond a "we don't do things that way" explanation.

Fear is such a broad term, encompassing many different states of mind. My fear felt like an unwillingness to give something up. So what was I afraid to give up? I didn't know. It was so frustrating to have a sense of something that I could not explain. The alarm going off in me was not a childlike, visceral reaction to the dark; it was a much more muddied feeling of which I had little conscious experience. I wasn't going to figure this emotion out in one sitting nor from one conversation.

TWO LESSONS LEARNED

I learned two important lessons from my engagement with Mara. First, I learned that I could have a conversation with someone who adamantly disagreed with me without the conversation getting heated or disagreeable. Though I invested a lot of emotional energy into the conversation, I didn't end up suffering any lingering wounds from her words or our interaction. The dialog, though it became quite academic, was in no way argumentative.

This lesson surprised me, because atheists and Christians have become quite polarized, viewing each other almost as different species rather than as friends and fellow thinkers. In prepping for our conversation, I had prepared for battle with an alien species who was invading my worldview, no doubt a learned behavior from the church as well as from the New Atheist movement (since I didn't have this view of atheism before my church life). Instead, the conversation turned out to be two thinking, feeling human beings rigorously engaging thoughts on their own views of the world. Mara didn't quit teaching my flute students after our interaction, nor did she avoid me. Rather, we engaged in even more chitchat, although she didn't pursue our religious conversation much.

Second, I learned that I didn't want to be a public Christian. I came from a culture in which religion was seen as a private matter. My experience with public Christians had been marred by televangelists and Hollywood portrayals of clergy or of unattainable sainthood figures like Mother Teresa and Billy Graham. I knew relatively little about the public options in between these two extremes. I was repulsed by the televangelists who, to me, represented corruption. Further, I had no desire to be at the level of a Billy Graham in sharing the gospel, nor did I think God chose many people to do such saintly activities. For me, a religious life lived quietly and respectfully, away from people, was my preferred option. And this revelation bothered me, for I knew it was against the model of the earliest disciples. The disciples told people about Jesus. They did so at the peril of their own lives. Here I was in the modern world, with all my comforts and freedoms, and I didn't even want to stand up for my beliefs.

The second lesson continued to haunt me as I tried to brush it off and get on with my semester, both in graduate school and in my music teaching position. I was scandalized by the thought that I wouldn't publicly stand up for what I believed. I'd never been that kind of person. I'd always stood up for what I believed in. *But this is different. Religious people are weird, fanatical, no less. You don't want to be associated with such a radical group. You know better than to do such a thing. You're a smart girl.* I couldn't believe the ridiculousness of my thoughts. I wasn't a well-known anybody. What did I think would happen if I began to take a stand for Christianity? My friends and family knew that I had become a Christian, but that was my private choice. If I were to trot out my beliefs in front of everyone online, I assumed they'd think I'd been brainwashed and become "one of those fundamentalists." I also figured that by standing up publicly I'd draw some nasty, unfriendly fire.

After arguing with myself for several months, I decided that once again I had overanalyzed the situation. I had almost convinced myself that all these musings about public Christianity were a waste of time. I had a career and was doing well. I didn't need to mess things up. We already struggled financially from low-paying ministry and teaching positions as well as from putting ourselves through college. So why would I think that God might want me to go into public ministry? Wasn't getting this apologetics degree risky enough?

I felt as though I stood on the edge of a cliff and was contemplating jumping off to see if God was really there. The ledge was solid and comforting. I could control what happened if I stayed on the ledge. To jump off and to see if my beliefs held up, as well as if God held me up, was lunacy. It was frightening because it would be a loss of control I was used to having over my life. Even so, I could not get past the idea that if my beliefs were worth a flying fig, I should be able to defend them thoughtfully and respectfully in public.

That November, I gave in and took the jump . . . perhaps, one might call it, a leap of faith. I began the Confident Christianity blog.

• CONSIDERATIONS •

1. Why is the resurrection of Jesus central to Christian faith?
2. How do you view the evidence of the resurrection? Is it convincing? Why or why not?
3. Why is it important to be relational and focus on the other person when arguing for God's existence?
4. Why do some people struggle with being open with others about what they believe?

CHAPTER 5

LESSONS FROM A

SOCIOPATH AND

AN EX-MUSLIM

Because our expression is imperfect we need friendship
to fill up the imperfections.

—G. K. CHESTERTON, *ILLUSTRATED LONDON NEWS*, JUNE 6, 1931

"At this point in the story, most people move away."

"Well, I'm not going anywhere."

David half-smiled at my response to his remark as he sat next
to me in a booth at a small dive of a Mexican restaurant in La
Mirada, California. It was the end of the first week of the apologetics graduate school summer program, and I had recently met
a couple of fellow students, David and Nabeel, who grabbed my
interest with their story of friendship and faith. Both guys stood
over six feet tall and had personalities as big as their stature. I had

agreed to go to a matinee movie and lunch with several students from the graduate program, and David was one of them. During lunch, I asked David about his background, a tale so fantastic that it could be its own television crime series, which is why he made his remark.

David Wood was a PhD candidate in philosophy. He was also a sociopath who went to jail for five years after he attempted to murder his father. In jail, David met a Christian inmate, Randy, who greatly annoyed him, due to David's arrogant form of atheism. He became especially angry when Randy tried to witness to him. In attempting to disprove God's existence to Randy, David ended up becoming a Christian.

David was quite intriguing or, perhaps, perplexing. I didn't know what to think about him. Should I believe his story? Should I try to get to know him better? Since I'd never met anyone like him, there was no way I could put him into a tidy personality box. He was a person whom I would never expect to be a Christian. I'd heard stories from former drug addicts, abusers, and criminals whose lives were drastically changed by trusting in Jesus, but never anything like this. David became a Christian, but he was still a sociopath. How should I interpret something like that? As our group made our way back to the car, one of the guys, Keith, mentioned that he'd like to take us out to dinner that night. I quickly agreed to his proposal, thinking, *I'm going to have another chance to figure out this David guy.*

That night, as Keith rolled up in his convertible PT Cruiser to my summer apartment near campus, I noticed that sitting next to David was his friend Nabeel Qureshi, an ex-Muslim from a Pakistani-American family. I had met Nabeel at the opening banquet, but I hadn't spoken with him since. Both he and David were scrunched into the small backseat of the car. After I offered to sit in back, and all the guys protested, I hopped in the front seat and away we went to a restaurant Keith had researched.

During our meal, I remained as quiet as possible, answering questions as asked and engaging in small talk here and there. I didn't want to appear too anxious nor too aloof, but I was a bit intimidated, especially by David and Nabeel's fast-paced, audacious banter. Plus, these guys had some serious background stories, whereas I felt my background wasn't anything fantastic in comparison. In between all David and Nabeel's joking with each other—which was oddly endearing—I discovered these two Christians were extremely committed to their belief in Jesus. These guys were "all in" for King Jesus, and most of their conversation focused on their interactions with Muslims and atheists. I found myself smiling as I watched their friendship unfold.

Finally, David turned to me, apparently wanting a bit more contribution from my side of the table. "So, Mary Jo, who is your favorite philosopher?"

Panic! Why is he asking me about this? I'm just a first-year apologetics student with a background in music education. I managed to eke out a few words. "I find myself drawn to Nietzsche.[1] I like the way he thinks, oh, and his writing style. Plus, he seems to really try to live out what he believes." My answer seemed pretty decent for semi-panic mode.

David raised one eyebrow, leaned forward, and bellowed, "Nietzsche! What do you know of Nietzsche?"

Well, that was unexpected. Most people just posture when it comes to backing their knowledge. Doesn't this guy understand the rules of the game? You don't ask people questions like that. Those are supposed to be unstated assumptions. My mind filed through

---

1 Nietzsche doesn't rank at the very top of my philosophers anymore.

years of comebacks that I had learned growing up in a quick-witted family. I hastily found something to throw back at him.

I leaned into the table to match his posturing. "What should I know of Nietzsche as a first-year apologetics student? Obviously not as much as *you*, right? Philosophy major!"

David smirked at the comment and leaned back in his chair. "Ha! I like that. She's fun."

Nabeel noticed my discomfort and moved the conversation in a new direction, asking me about my music background. I appreciated his graciousness, but I didn't want to move the conversation toward small talk. After a short response to him, I quickly turned the conversation back to David. "Why are you here with Nabeel? You aren't in classes."

"I'm prepping for a debate with an atheist guy. I thought it would be good to get away and spend my days studying while Nabeel goes to class." Though I knew Nabeel was an ex-Muslim, I didn't know he was a new believer at that time. David had encouraged him to get a Christian education, which is why they were both at the school. David thought the apologetics degree would be a good place to start, and he came along to support Nabeel.

"Oh, you do debates? Do you mean public debates? Is there a way I could watch this one online?"

"That's what I mean. Me and Nabeel are starting a ministry, Anastasis Apologetics." Nabeel moved his head closer to me and said, "That's a fancy Greek word for resurrection, and, yes, we'll upload our upcoming debate onto our webpage."

"Would you guys mind if I watched the debate and sent you my thoughts?"

David raised his eyebrow again. "Sure. If it's any good, maybe we'll post your review to our website."

"Great," I responded coolly with just a twinge of excitement. These Christian men weren't blowing me off, changing the subject, or alienating me, attitudes I had unfortunately grown to expect among evangelicals. These guys seemed to really be interested in my analysis of their arguments.

Later, when the time finally came for me to hand over the review, I had second thoughts. David had a website called Answering Infidels through which he handled a lot of the arguments from another site, Internet Infidels, dedicated to promoting atheist views. He was going to post my response on this site that got quite a bit of attention from atheists. *You don't want attention like that. You're going to have to spend all your time responding to criticisms and attacks.*

I then began to understand my fears about public Christianity. I feared losing autonomy and control. To enter the public arena meant responsibility to engage with others. In the marketplace of ideas, there are unspoken rules. If you take a stand on something publicly, you've got to be willing to respond to at least some of the criticism. Though I was no stranger to smaller, localized leadership roles, I had no desire to set up such a public target on my back. I was worried that I wouldn't be able to just continue doing whatever I wanted with my small, unknown blog. I would bear a new responsibility to handle these criticisms. Further, I was giving up, in part, the ability to control public perception of me. Others could say whatever they wanted of me, and there wasn't much I could do about it.

I took a last look at some of David and Nabeel's responses to others online. The guys seemed to be holding their own. *I can do this . . . Lord, I hope I'm supposed to do this. I'm trusting you to let me know.* After several assessments of what I'd written, I passed the review along to David, who promptly posted it on his website.

Public engagement didn't trickle in nicely, a little at a time, so I could dip my feet in and try things out. Rather, a wave of engagement carried me right into the thick of things. I began to spend much of my nights answering objections to my review. Further, I didn't just receive criticisms but also began to receive requests for help with doubts. It was exactly what I feared would happen. Before I got involved with David and Nabeel's ministry, I felt like I was the captain of my own ship. After just a few interactions with their ministry, I felt like my ship was drastically changing course . . . because it was.

BROADENING MY VIEW

David and Nabeel began to partner with me in putting together debates. Roger loved that I had found a couple of Christian friends who scooped me up and brought me alongside them. The guys would fly me out to Norfolk, Virginia, to help them organize, administrate, and host the debates. While I was content to assist with just the administrative aspects, neither of them was going to let me stay in that role for long. They placed me in the spotlight more and more, taking me from debate host to debate timekeeper to debate moderator. Finally, David and Nabeel challenged me to a debate with a Muslim man, which I ended up doing in 2009 in Dearborn, Michigan, as part of The Great Debate series. The debate was titled "Did Jesus Die on the Cross?" Afterwards, David posted the debate on their website, Acts 17 Apologetics, with the caption, "Yes, we have a girl debater."

Hanging out with these two on-fire Christians was almost otherworldly. Each time we got together was like being transported out of the world I knew into something so foreign to me. The guys had focused their ministries on answering Muslims, and so we engaged mostly in evangelizing and debating Muslims, as well as in apologetics events geared toward responding to Islam. We even participated in a satellite television show, *Jesus or Muhammad*, that was broadcast as far as the Middle East. It was crazy. I grew up in a culture that seemed so far away from all the cultural issues we dealt with in ministering to Muslims.

One afternoon we were driving to such a ministry event in Michigan. I was sitting in the backseat with the guys sitting upfront. Nabeel's phone rang, as it did quite frequently. He glanced to see who was calling and then picked up the call. The conversation immediately became a mixture of Urdu and English and also became noticeably edgy. I could hear a woman's voice on the other end: Nabeel's mom. After fifteen or so minutes, the call abruptly ended.

We all sat quiet for a moment. Then David turned his focus to rapping some eighties tune. Nabeel was still quiet and not moving. I couldn't see his face, but I could feel his tension. It was an emotional conversation. Every time I saw him take calls from his family, I saw his jovial demeanor drop into one of deep anguish. I sat behind him, not knowing what to offer. David switched into beatboxing.

In that moment, traveling some highway to some event where we were off to minister to people I didn't know, in a cultural environment in which I felt grossly out of place, time seemed to stand still. I had been nervous about the event, but the weight of that phone call effectively dampened my emotions. Nabeel began to check his text messages, a soothing habit for him. I mused about his situation. Here was a man who decided to follow what he thought was true, and it cost him one of the most precious things in life, his own family. When I became a Christian, I probably lost some intellectual and emotional ground with family members, but it was not even comparable to the loss Nabeel had experienced or the betrayal the Qureshi family felt.

My whole life I'd grown up with a "live and let live" attitude. My family may not believe something, but we respected the choices of others who did. I had never seen anything up close and personal like Nabeel's sacrifice. *So the world isn't such a safe place for a diversity of ideas, after all. Some people are not interested in a "live and let live" attitude. And they do not think there's anything wrong with that. They may even think they have a better commitment to their beliefs. How did I miss this fact?* I had been so worried about myself that I hadn't considered what taking a stand was like for others, especially those who risked their most precious relationships. My family may have been disappointed or confused by my conversion, but they weren't devastated. We still had good relationships. When I saw the torment of Nabeel's family, I understood, for the first time, just how sheltered my life had been. The Qureshi family was a microcosm of whole people groups around the world whose religious beliefs were the most sacred thing in their lives, and who were unwilling to sacrifice their respective worldviews for anything. To them, the meaning of tolerance was closer to "giving up their own view" than simply "putting up with others' views." Some things were just not tolerable.

"Was that your mom?" I finally asked.

"Yeah."

"How is she?"

"The same."

"I'm sorry. I don't know what to say. I have no experience with this kind of thing."

"Don't worry, MJ. It's just the way things are right now."

We sat in anguished silence for several minutes while David

continued beatboxing. Nabeel turned toward me. "By the way, I think you'd get along with my parents."

There it is . . . that optimism. Nabeel was a guy who was ever hopeful and loved to laugh. And if he could use a tense moment for some lighthearted sarcasm, he was extra pleased with himself.

I chuckled and began to think of a snarky comeback but paused. *He's actually hurting under that sarcasm, and he's got an event to do . . . just let it alone.* I decided to change to another subject that greatly concerned me. "So, what's this I hear about you guys receiving threats . . . death threats?"

David abruptly stopped beatboxing and focused on my question, looking at me in the rearview mirror. "Yeah, check it out. Me and Nabeel were arguing with this Muslim guy online. It was totally legit. We were getting into the deity of Christ. At first, it was just chill. Nabeel was sort of hanging out in the background of the conversation. Once Nabeel heard this guy's case claiming that Jesus doesn't say, 'I'm God, worship me,' anywhere in the Bible, he jumped in and started laying down bombs."

Nabeel perked up. "I couldn't let the guy just ignore passages where Jesus claims to be God, just because he doesn't use those exact words. I mean, where does Jesus say, 'I'm only a prophet; don't worship me!' He doesn't say those exact words, either, but he does make a lot of claims that only God can make." Nabeel began a list, counting each claim on his fingers.

1. Jesus claimed to be the "I AM" of the Exodus 3:14 in John 8:24 and 8:58.
2. Jesus claimed to be Lord of the Sabbath in Mark 2:28.
3. Jesus claimed to be the apocalyptic "Son of Man" from Daniel 7:13–14 in Mark 14:62.

4. Jesus claimed to be able to forgive sins in Luke 7:40–50.

5. Jesus claimed to be able to answer prayers in John 14:13–14.

6. Jesus claimed to be greater than the temple of God in Matthew 12:6.

"And I'm just warming up."

David laid out a beatbox background to the rhythm of Nabeel's evidence list. Both guys now began to turn the evidences into some kind of crazy rap tune, taking turns at the Scripture.

Ha! This is why I hang out with these two. They're hilarious.

"Well, uh, guys, that's really awesome, but how does this relate to the death threats?"

David once again abruptly stopped his singing and said, "As soon as Nabeel began to throw down arguments, some of the Muslims who'd been watching the dialog unfold online started to chime in more aggressively. They tend to get more aggravated when an apostate, such as Nabeel, gets involved."

"What kinds of things did they say?"

"They said if they ever saw us in public, they kill us."

"What did you say in response?"

David looked at me, smiled sheepishly, and said, "I corrected their poor grammar. 'If you're going to write threats, at least learn to do it with proper English.'"

"Oh, man, you didn't do that, did you, David?"

David paused, smiled, and resolutely said, "Yes, I did."

The guys quickly picked up their song. Amid the atmosphere of levity, I sat there stunned. *It's only an internet threat. It doesn't really mean anything . . . does it?* I couldn't make sense of why someone would threaten a person's life for disagreeing on religious views. I had no experience with this kind of thing, and I was distressed at what I heard. I sat in the back of the car, looking at the passing Michigan scenery, trying to process their words.

Nabeel, noticing my silence, said, "Don't worry, Jo."

"But I am worried. I don't know much about Islam, nor Muslims. This is my first experience with the Muslim community. I mean, in my conversations with atheists, they call me horrible names, but they don't threaten me."

"Well, I don't want you to think it's indicative of all Muslims. It's not. Most Muslims in the world are not violent people. Take my family, for instance. We would never threaten anyone like that, nor would any of the families I grew up with." Nabeel paused for a moment, trying to find the right words to say. "It's actually a pretty complicated matter. On the one hand, Muslims are quite varied in their views and beliefs, just like you'd find in any other worldview. Plus, Muslims are individuals, so even within different sects, there are variations of what people know and what they believe. It's possible to find everything from passive to radical views under the umbrella of Islam.

"On the other hand, part of my own journey out of Islam included discovering some of the calls to violence that I read in the Qur'an and in the life of Muhammad. Though I was shocked to find them—and at first I tried to explain them away—I couldn't deny that those passages were in the texts and in the history of Islam. Part of my crisis of faith came from recognizing that though most of the Muslims I knew were peaceful, Muhammad himself was not."

I thought about what Nabeel had offered. "Well, I'm afraid that by even asking that question I'll get labeled as Islamophobic, but I have concerns."

David chimed in. "Uh, you're not even close to Islamophobia, which means the *irrational* fear of Islam or of Muslims. That word is misused and abused. To have concerns based on the teachings of Muhammad is not the same thing as irrationally fearing a worldview or a people."

"Though, David," Nabeel interjected, "I'd say that some people are unnecessarily fearful of Muslims. Jo, you just need to sit down with some Muslim families and share dinner with them. I think that would alleviate your concern. Actually, I think that would help a lot of people toward understanding their Muslim friends and neighbors better. And you'd get some pretty awesome food!"

Of course, Nabeel brought up food. In my years of ministry with Nabeel, he was always goading me on to try new foods, especially anything Pakistani. Anyone who knew Nabeel knew he loved sharing meals.

Nabeel wasn't finished with the matter. "But I don't want to downplay the major differences I found between Muhammad and Jesus. Think about these passages from the Qur'an." He then began to quote Surah 4:89: "They but wish that ye should reject Faith, as they do, and thus be on the same footing (as they): But take not friends from their ranks until they flee in the way of God (from what is forbidden). But if they turn renegades, seize them and slay them wherever ye find them; and (in any case) take no friends or helpers from their ranks."

I later found a book called *The Crisis of Islam* by Bernard Lewis, a Near Eastern studies scholar at Princeton. In the book, Lewis explained the outworking of this passage into Islamic law, noting, "The renegade is the one who has known the true faith, however briefly, and abandoned it. For this offense there is no human forgiveness, and according to the overwhelming majority of the jurists, the renegade must be put to death—that is, if male."[2]

---

2   Bernard Lewis, *The Crisis of Islam* (New York: Random House, 2003), 41.

Nabeel continued with a verse from one of the last books of the Qur'an. This status of being one of the last books is important because of the Islamic rule of abrogation, the rule that a later verse is to replace an earlier verse if there is any contradiction. Therefore, this is one of the last teachings of the Qur'an. He recited Surah 9:29: "Fight those who believe not [in Islam] . . . (even if they are) of the People of the Book [Christians and Jews], until they pay the Jizya with willing submission, and feel themselves subdued." He paused and then said, "Now follow these verses with Surah 3:32, 'Allah does not love the unbelievers.' Add in to the mix that Muhammad himself led bloody military campaigns. If someone wants to find a reason for threatening my life, they can find it in Muhammad's own words and deeds."

He continued, "But contrast that with what we know about Jesus and his teachings." And he outlined the following Scriptures:

- 1 John 4:19–21—"We love because he [God] first loved us. If anyone says, 'I love God,' and hates his brother, he is a liar; for he who does not love his brother whom he has seen cannot love God whom he has not seen. And this commandment we have from him: whoever loves God must also love his brother."
- Matthew 5:43–44—"You have heard that it was said, 'You shall love your neighbor and hate your enemy.' But I say to you, Love your enemies and pray for those who persecute you."
- Romans 5:8—"But God shows his love for us in that while we were still sinners, Christ died for us."

Nabeel concluded, "Jesus actually taught us to love our

enemies and do good to them. The Bible explains that love is from God and anyone who says they love God must also love their brother. And we're all basically brothers and sisters on this earth. Plus, we didn't have to show God love first before he sacrificed for us. This is much different from Allah not loving the unbelievers or his commanding the unbelievers be put to death. And those things, along with all the study I did on the resurrection of Jesus, really changed my heart about who God is and what he's like."

David was now trying to get our attention as we approached the event venue. He didn't know the exact address, so Nabeel went searching through the emails on his phone to find it. While they were occupied, I replayed some of Nabeel's words in my mind. *Why have I never encountered these aspects of Islam before? What do I even know about other religions and cultures of the world? It feels like I know nothing. Why was my education so deficient?*

We arrived at our event a little late, but overall the conference went well. Throughout the night, I met numerous believers who had left Islam to the disdain and threats of their families. These people were willing to give everything up to follow Jesus— literally, everything. Once again, I found myself lacking the background to process such a choice. I wish I could say that my response was admiration for their sacrifice and boldness, but my response was muted. I didn't know that life, I didn't want that life, and I feared giving up my own way of being. I was very unlike many of the people I met in this ministry. Their culture was so different from the culture of the Pacific Northwest.

Standing off in a corner of the conference hall, watching the conference attendees socialize, hoping no one would talk to me, I remembered a scenic turnout sign on the Oregon Coast that had been graffitied with the phrase, "There, you've seen it. Now, go home." This one phrase, for me, embodied the culture in which I was raised. We cared for our little piece of the world. We recycled and were passionate about leaving a small carbon footprint. But back then, I was young and did not yet have a global perspective. I could definitely say that I really didn't care about the rest of the world as long as I could walk on the beach, hike to the top of the waterfall, and camp in pristine forests away from others.

David and Nabeel taught me, in a real and lasting way, that people and God were more important than having my own little haven in the way I wanted to have it. In ministering with these two sold-out believers, I began to see the selfishness of my heart in a striking array of self-focused, excuse-driven, white-suburbanite American detail. *There are so many other ways of being in the world.* I had always been taught that the people of the world are more alike than different—essentially, yes. However, such differences as I'd discovered were not the kind that are easily reconciled by "just loving one another."

My experience of the church had been a menagerie of disappointment, marginalization, and isolation, with very few glimpses of the original beauty that drew me to God. I knew nearly nothing of what it was like in Christianity to be accepted for who you actually are. Then David and Nabeel came crashing into my life with immediate confidence about what they saw in me. They weren't afraid to let me lead or put me on stage in public. Rather, they seemed to relish times when they could sit in the front row at one of my presentations and make faces at me to see if they could throw me off course. They listened to me when I critiqued them, they valued my opinion, and they implemented what I said. Their demeanor with me challenged my whole view of what I was doing in Christianity.

David and Nabeel's friendship also challenged my introversion. They had a completely different way of looking at the world. Whereas my heart broke for the evil I saw and so I spent time alone in lament, these guys rushed into the middle of things. Their response to heartbreak was to bring as many people to God as possible. The more I partnered with them, the more relativism I shed, and specifically, my "live and let live" attitude. I also began to see that I had focused so much on the problems I saw in the church that I hadn't recognized my own failings in my relationship with it.

My heart was changing. *It's okay to stand up for things I believe are true. It's okay to completely disagree with others. It's okay to experience offensive and degrading comments from others. It's okay to not respond in a derogatory manner to verbally abusive people. It's okay to trust God with all these things and with my life, both spiritual and physical. I don't have to like it, but it's okay.*

With the encouragement of my husband, these guys pushed me out of my comfort zone and truly gave me an initial, and somewhat abrupt, start in apologetics ministry. I had no real idea what I was doing or where I was going, so I let these two giant personalities lead. And where they led me was straight into more public debates.

• CONSIDERATIONS •

1. How has your background been an influence in how you live as a Christian in public?
2. What have you had to give up, or what would you have to give up, in order to follow Christ? How is that thing a deterrent to you in searching for truth?
3. How does the existence of multiple religious and atheistic views affect your view of God?
4. Have you ever encountered Christians who had such an impact on your life as to transform your way of thinking or living? If so, what was that experience and why did it so greatly impact you?

CHAPTER 6

DEBATING GOOD AND EVIL

The atheist who argues from worldly suffering, even crudely, against belief in God both benevolent and omnipotent is still someone whose moral expectations of God—and moral disappointments—have been shaped at the deepest level by the language of Christian faith.

—DAVID BENTLEY HART, *THE DOORS OF THE SEA*

"Listen, the argument from evil is only as forceful as the suffering that exists in this present world. If there was no intense suffering, the argument would lose most of its force. If there was no suffering at all, then it would have no force at all."

I read the atheist debater's statement over and over. Visions of poverty-stricken villages from UNICEF commercials and war-torn cities from the nightly news popped into my head. The Green River Killer, the Branch Davidian standoff, the AIDS epidemic, the Holocaust of the Second World War, and a flood of other tragedies crowded my thoughts. My intention was to offer a rebuttal, but I wasn't so sure I had anything to refute here. *He's right. If there was no evil or suffering, would anyone really question God's goodness or sovereignty? Or if so, what kind of power/impact would their argument have in a world void of evil and suffering?*

The gentleman was responding to my written review of his dialog with David. After I promised a review of David's next debate, I discovered the next debate was an informal dialog on a podcast titled *The Debate Hour.* I wrote a review of the dialog, which David posted to his website. David's dialog partner responded on his own blog. As I sat at my computer, poised to continue my refutations, I lingered on this one statement.

What should I say in reply? Anything I offered was going to sound too simplistic and distant in light of the depth of individual suffering and pain. For even my own painful experiences in the church had come to no resolution, and there was no end in sight to our ministry problems. My analytic side kept moralizing that I knew the reasons there was suffering in the world, but my emotions would not be swayed by logic, nor was I sure that they should. Therefore, I argued with myself that I couldn't respond, appealing to the fact that I didn't really know suffering and pain, not like the suffering I had read about or seen on TV. And even while I argued with myself, my arguments highlighted the frustration I had with the church.

If others were indeed suffering so much, why had I come across so many Christians who seemed disinterested in their pain? Hadn't Jesus taught us to take care of the poor, sick, naked, hungry, thirsty, and imprisoned (Matthew 25:35–45)? Why, then, were arguments over the church carpet color and whether jeans could be worn on stage more prevalent than how we could best serve our communities? Perhaps my view was colored by the position I held as a music minister's wife, in which I saw all the inner workings of specific churches. Still, this sting of hypocrisy deeply wounded my heart.

The sting is why I have such a dual reaction to arguments against God based on the existence of suffering in the world. On the one hand, I recoil at those who believe Christians are either unaware of suffering or inept in their explanation for its severity. On the other hand, I find myself agreeing strongly with the arguer who laments that life "shouldn't be this way."

For example, the debater suggested,

> Neither Sharp [me] nor Wood [my friend David] can actually see the blood-stained whip in the slave master's hand, nor smell the flesh of the witches burned at the stake, nor hear the screams of the woman whose child is eaten alive by a pack of wolves, because they are blinded by their faith. They cover their eyes, their noses, and their ears to the truth of this world in order to have the comforts of a delusional belief.

I would agree that I have no experience with any of these situations, nor do many people growing up in the United States in my generation. It would be disingenuous and inconsiderate to say I know what those things are like. I have only my own experiences, which I hoped would help me to understand suffering to some degree. I have felt the pain of marginalization, isolation, and depression, and I have personally experienced the lack of concern for the poor and needy . . . and all within church ministry. So, for this debater to paint me as a happy, small-minded churchgoer was unfortunate at best, vain at worst. Just because I hadn't experienced the horrors he described was no good reason to believe I was blind to the suffering of the world, or that I hadn't undergone suffering of my own. And I could have turned the argument on the arguer. But I wanted a better answer to his charge . . . for myself.

"He's right, you know."

Roger sat down on the sofa, exhausted already from an emotional day in church ministry. "Who's right, Jo?"

I had a habit of entering into a conversation with Roger as if he were running alongside the thoughts in my head. "The debater. He's right in saying that the argument from evil is only as forceful as the suffering in the world."

"Oh, you're talking about David's debate?"

"Yeah. I mean, everyone on earth will suffer in some way or another. I understand that suffering is the cost of human autonomy, when free will is used destructively. But it's one thing to talk about it, and quite another to suffer greatly."

"You've worked on this problem for a while now. You've argued that the evil in the world is the result of man using his free will in destructive ways."

"Have I worked on it? *Have I really?* It seems so harsh, almost unreal. It just feels so unsatisfying in light of the amount and extent of suffering in the world. Think about all the suffering inflicted on others because some world leader thought what they were doing was 'right.' Think about all the things that happen on a daily basis, in which someone is treated with disrespect, or a person feels so unloved as to commit suicide. Even just our own encounters in church . . . I don't think anyone there set out to do what was *evil*; they thought they were *right*. It's so much to take in. And I'm fairly certain I cannot even fathom what I'm talking about."

Roger looked amused, if not a slight bit annoyed. "Are you having a good conversation with yourself over there?"

"Hey, I'm serious."

"Yeah, you're seriously into your own head right now. I was just wondering if you really needed me here."

"I just get so angry about this issue. Why don't more people think on this matter? Why did I never learn about the problem of suffering and pain from the church? Why do atheist debaters think they have to shame other debaters into truly considering this matter? Maybe they had similar experiences to mine in church. I don't know. There's so much unhelpful *everything* going on!" Once again, I found myself unable to express my emotions, much less my ideas.

"Okay, well, 'unhelpful everything' isn't a thing, and you seem really agitated about this guy's response."

"Yes, I'm agitated. On the one hand, it seems to me that this is a good argument. How do you argue against personal suffering and pain? Even if I think I have a reasoned argument, couldn't someone just say, 'You don't know anything about *my* suffering,' and then I'd be left to agree with them. What good does it do to tell someone *why* there is suffering *when* they are suffering? But on the other hand, if all suffering is reduced to subjective experiences of it, then what do we even mean by the word *suffering*? Since every instance of it would be different, we'd have nothing by which we could say, 'This is what we mean by suffering.' The word would be stripped of its meaning. The whole endeavor would be a delusion. We'd be left with nothing to say. One man's suffering would be another man's good day, and vice versa ad nauseum."

Roger nodded, searching for what to say.

I continued. "I just don't know what to do about all the evil in the world. And I get a little upset when debaters roll out this argument with a morally superior sneer of indignation toward Christians who are trying to make sense of the argument and who are trying to offer hope. The debater said his solution is that we should all learn to treat each other better. Really? That easy, huh? Hey . . . all you suckers throughout time and history, you just didn't get the memo: treat each other better. You know, show love, not hate."

I continued. "Here's the real kicker: we humans seem to be the problem. With all our knowledge, advancements, and resources, we keep doing the wrong things . . . even when we try to do what we think is right. These guys seem to think that we humans—the problem—can also be the solution. Twenty centuries of being the problem gives me little hope that our solutions are going to be stellar in the next twenty centuries."

Roger finally interjected a remark. "It's not really up to you to fix all the world's problems."

"Yeah, I just feel so insignificant in what I'm doing. So what if I made an argument that demonstrates why there is evil in the world . . . how much good did that do? Today, so many people will be raped, murdered, sold into slavery, beaten, die of disease, overdose on drugs, or starve. It's beyond heartbreaking."

"But it sounds like you have no hope. What's the hope, Jo?"

"If it's not Jesus, then we're all wrecked, now, aren't we? If there is no God, no moral obligations or objective moral values, then what you see is what you get. I've seen that we're not progressing over the years. The twentieth century was the bloodiest century of human history. We're using our rationality and ingenuity to become more efficient and creative in how we destroy one another. We're using our knowledge and resources to practice mass manipulation for political power. And we do so under the guise of being 'inclusive.' But we're not inclusive; we've become more polarized and less thoughtful. And the people just join up with their parties, and marginalize the other party, without a care for how marginalization leads to dehumanizing."

"Wow. That's a lot, Jo. You got all that from one sentence from the debate review?"

"Yeah."

"So what are you going to do about it?"

"Talk to someone else." I laughed when I saw his relief. Roger has been so great at listening to me over the years, but sometimes I need to give him a break as sparring partner.

BACK TO DR. JONES

The summer before that debate, the same summer I met David and Nabeel, we had a special topics class with Dr. Clay Jones on the problem of evil. So far, I'd only read and heard scholars approach this issue from a fairly dry palette. The arguments were logical, and actually quite useful, but I kept finding people who would say, "Yeah, but what about the suffering of X," concerning themselves or another. The logical arguments didn't seem to resonate emotionally with many people. I would argue that there's no logical contradiction between God's existence and the presence of evil in the world, but the question kept coming back to a personalization of certain instances of suffering. While philosopher Alvin Plantinga demonstrates in *God, Freedom, and Evil* that there is still no logical contradiction between God and instances of suffering (no matter how great), I just couldn't find a better way to talk about suffering. I was ready to hear another perspective.

Dr. Jones began his talk, which he called "Witch Hunts, Inquisitions, and Crusades."[1] *That's kind of blunt. Is this really*

---

1   Some people will cite these three examples as archetype behavior by Christians in history. It doesn't take much digging to discover the error in this way of thinking. See chapter 6 in "Further Resources" found at the end of this book.

an objection to Christianity? Little did I know that this kind of argument, pointing out evil committed at the hands of professing Christians, was hugely popular. Jones took us through the historical facts surrounding these events, demythologizing each one. Then he talked about why these things happen in the first place. He said something I've never forgotten: "We say such atrocities are inhumane. Is this inhumane . . . or in-human? No, this is what humans do." Jones explained that these horrible acts were committed by human beings because human beings are the kind of thing that commits horrible acts. He then warned us that his talk was about to get much rougher. *And it did.* Jones laid out the atrocities of humankind over the centuries . . . in detail. These examples were so horrifying that it was hard to wrap my mind around some of them: the Rwandan genocide, the live burial of Confucian philosophers, the man-made famine-genocide in Ukraine.

Here I was, living in early twenty-first century America, relatively clueless on the actual atrocities of humankind. I knew a few of them, but I'd never taken time to study such things in detail. *Who does that, anyway? Why subject yourself to such horrors?* Jones said these things were important to know because we don't understand how truly awful "average" human beings can be, and so we don't understand the problem of evil.

When I had a chance, I decided to dig a little deeper with Dr. Jones on this very issue. So I picked a time that worked for both of us and jumped into my questions.

"Hey, Dr. Jones! I'm really struggling to understand why more people, especially in the church, don't take the problem of evil more seriously. I have a few questions for you about your work in this area."

"Yeah, I'd be glad to help in any way I can. Go ahead."

I leaned back into my chair and began. "You have a lecture

during which you say over and over, 'Is this inhumane?' And then you respond to yourself, 'No, this is what humans do.' So, what is it you mean when you say that we, as humans, don't understand the depth of our evil?"

"Well, you put it pretty well right there. We do not understand the depth of our evil. And one of the ways I put it is that we were all born Auschwitz-enabled."

"That sounds pretty harsh. What do you mean by that?"

"Well, let me go back a bit to how I got to that conclusion. About, oh, I don't know, twenty years ago, I began to study genocide. And the only reason that I began to study genocide, frankly, was I didn't want anyone to say, 'You really didn't look at human evil very deeply; you haven't looked at how horrific it really is.'"

This is exactly the argument leveled against David and me from the debater: that we turn a blind eye to the suffering of humankind.

"I was actually looking for a good quote, something really horrific about someone murdering children or raping people. Then I could say, 'See, that's how bad it is, let's get to the argument.' Well, then I began instead to really look at this stuff. I started reading entire books on human evil. One of the first ones to grip me was *The Rape of Nanking* by Iris Chang, about what happened in Nanking, China, in 1937. An estimated 380,000 women were raped by soldiers. These soldiers went beyond rape to disembowel women, slice off their breasts, and nail them alive to walls. Anyway, I kept reading similar books, and one day—I think it was while I had *The Rape of Nanking* in my hand—I thought, 'This is what humans do! Humans do genocide.'"

Jones seemed to be saying that it wasn't the "monster" of a person that would partake in such evil, but the average human being. But his conclusion didn't seem right. All my life, I had believed humans were basically good and would do good things given the right circumstances. I think this is why I struggled so much with all the instances of human suffering around the world. It seemed so unfair that good people should have to endure such ugly and devastating situations. Realizing I was drifting in thought, I quickly snapped back to Jones's next words.

"Frankly, humans without that much provocation will rape, torture, and murder people if they think they can get away with it and if somehow they think it's in their best interest. It happens all the time."

Well, he's not wrong about that. If I watch the evening news on any given day, I see all those things.

"Another great book is *We Wish to Inform You That Tomorrow We Will Be Killed with Our Families: Stories from Rwanda.* It's about a Tutsi pastor, writing to the Hutu leader of his own Christian denomination, stating that if the Hutu leader doesn't come get them, they will be killed the very next day. The Hutu leader doesn't come, and they are killed. Now, in light of these stories, and all the genocide stories I read, there's one fact that stands out to me. Every genocide researcher I know says—and every genocide victim agrees—that *it's the average member of a population that commits genocide.*"

"That's why I came to the conclusion that we were all born Auschwitz-enabled. We need to understand what we mean by 'human goodness.' We know humans fantasize about committing adultery, fantasize about murdering people, and just generally hate people's guts. So why do they not act out on it? It's because of self-interest. When humans convince themselves that something is really in their own self-interest, they will act out on it. Humans are not good. But if you think humans are generally good, you'll have a hard time believing the doctrine of original sin—which is the only thing that explains why we were born Auschwitz-enabled. Christians don't want to talk about this because it's an ugly, gruesome subject, but I think they should, obviously."

PARADIGMS AND ALIEN JUDGES

We concluded our conversation, I thanked Dr. Jones for his time, and I left. In the next few days, as I tried to imagine the depth of pain, the horror of suffering that so many humans have inflicted on each other, I began to have that most unwelcome feeling of having my paradigm shifted. *Humans are not good. It's the average member of society that commits genocide.* I didn't want this to be true, and to this day I don't want it to be true. These ideas go against everything I believed growing up and into my young adulthood. But what if I were to be a defense lawyer in a trial of humanity where the judges were some alien race? As the prosecution brought forth the massive amounts of human suffering caused by other humans, what would I have to say? "Well, you see, Your Honor, I can tell you that at least I'm not like that . . . and neither is my family."

I could hear the alien judge: "You seem to forget yourself. The probability of your goodness is so infinitesimally low in light of human history, that I have no reason for judgment in your favor. Or perhaps you can prove that you are better than every human who has ever lived?"

"Well, no, I don't think I could do that, but there are some great humans in time and history: Mother Teresa, Martin Luther King Jr., Mahatma Gandhi . . ."

"And what percentage of humankind do they represent? Less than a percent? Less than half a percent? Less than half of a half of a percent? And can you prove that even those humans never did anything to hurt another human? You would do well to offer more realistic statements in your defense."

"But what explains all this? We have accomplished amazing things!"

The alien judge, looking unimpressed with my plea, says, "You seem to have an internal error."

There it was. Clay Jones's statement that we all suffer from original sin. And if he's right, no matter how averse our generation has become to the word *sin*, the answer to the problem is not more education, more opportunity, or more resources. None of these things can, *or have*, cured the lack of goodness in human beings. For all of the Enlightenment's work to show religion as false, or the language deconstruction that has relegated everything to the subjectivity of the individual, or the experimental drugs trying to release us to higher realities, or the sexual revolution trying to give us ultimate autonomy, or the new atheism movement that says we can be good without God . . . we are still full of selfishness, envy, hatred, racism, sexism, objectification, self-interest, and yet, self-loathing. We are not getting better. We can pretty up the terminology all we want, but the ugliness still rears its head in all of our lives.

Humanism: Beliefs stressing the potential value and goodness of human beings, attaching prime importance to human rather than divine or supernatural matters.

Adapted from Lexico, s.v. "humanism," www.lexico.com/en/definition/humanism.

Wow. I feel like I just raised a glass to toast my generation and gave the worst speech of all time. Honestly, I really do fit in better with the crowd that believes we should all "follow our dreams." But what is the cost of ignoring what I see? To blindly cling to a belief that humans are good despite the evidence? I had been raised with such **humanistic** optimism! *We all just need to respect each other, and the world will finally come together.* However, the empirical evidence, found in human history, suggests the complete opposite conclusion. No matter how good we think we are or how far along we think we've come, we're still doing horrible things to each other and to ourselves. I don't need to go to the historical atrocities to come to this conclusion. Becoming an adult was sufficient for me to understand that humans, on a daily basis, do not do what is good to each other. This idea was becoming plain as day through my experiences in church ministry. Even the people who professed the moral teachings of God as binding on their lives practiced nearly the worst of human behaviors and attitudes.

Where does all this leave me with the original objection? "The problem of evil is only as forceful as the suffering that exists." Yes, it does have force because of the suffering, but in what direction does that force push me? It could push me toward denying that a good God exists. If it did so, then I cannot be honest with myself by merely pontificating on that belief. I would have to embrace it as true . . . and all the resultant beliefs that go with it.

If a good God did not exist, the billions of humans committing what I would have called "evils" or "wrongful actions" against humankind would be oddly exonerated. For there would be no sin, no injustice, nothing out of the ordinary to call our experiences "suffering." Doesn't suffering imply that there's a way things are supposed to be? If this world, as we experience it, is just the way things are, then there's no grounding for saying that we are not as we are "supposed" to be. As I look back on human history, as I look into my own painful experiences in the church, I wonder if I'm ready to intellectually and emotionally commit to an ideology that would evaporate any injustice I had ever thought I found.

I am not ready to do so. I do believe there is such a thing as suffering. I do believe there is a way things should be and there are deviations from the standard. We call these deviations "evil," "wrong," "injustice," "suffering," or "hurt," depending on what kind of deviation from a standard of goodness they entail. Yet to believe these things are real deviations, I must figure out where I'm getting the standard to use for comparison. What is the thing throughout time and history that has given people an idea that there is a way things are *supposed to be*, no matter their cultural versions of expressing that standard?[2] The force of this question lies in the fact that all cultures assume there is a way that is "better" or "good." In looking at the available answers, I keep coming back to the Christian view of God as the source and standard of goodness. He would be an unchanging, consistent standard of goodness, because goodness is his nature. I even have an example of God demonstrating his goodness toward humankind by laying down his life for the sake of his creation.

Still, I hate to admit that human beings are not basically good. I want to believe the best about myself and others, despite the mountain of historical evidence that says we humans are not good. My aversion is not uncommon. Even C. S. Lewis said, "The greatest barrier I have met is the almost total absence from the minds of my audience of any sense of sin."[3]

Perhaps I could use the readily available excuse of blaming a certain set of people for the problems I see. *If we could just get*

---

2 Cultures may disagree about certain aspects of moral values (e.g., polygamy versus monogamy), yet they can also find agreements, like killing babies for fun is immoral. There is some standard beneath all our interpretations, since no one can completely avoid using a standard. We tend to argue about what the standard is and how it practically works out into human life (laws, customs, etc.).

3 C. S. Lewis, *God in the Dock* (Grand Rapids: Eerdmans, 1970), 243.

rid of religious followers. If we could just get rid of Communist dictators. If we could just get rid of neo-Nazis. If we could just get rid of racists. If we could just get rid of "haters." If we could just get rid of bad parents. If we could just get rid of people who are proud. If we could just get rid of envious people. But where would it end? If I keep going, my list would entail every human that has ever lived. My fictitious alien judge is correct. The problem comes back to each one of us. Yet I am not ready for this admission. Not only would it point back to me as part of the problem, but it would explain much of my problem with people in the church. And I'm not sure I want *those* problems explained in *that* way.

Ultimately, to the debater I say, *Yes, you're right. But the argument's force is what moves me back to belief that humans are not good and that God is still the answer. And if you think I'm being naive or irrational, what can I say to you? It is your prerogative to think so. I'm not sure I could convince you otherwise, since this is a debate that has persisted for years. But I am not convinced that injustice, suffering, and evil have no meaning, no grounding. For not only do I find that view incoherent within the framework of human experience, but I also find it unequipped to argue that human suffering itself is something real.*

And now I'm faced with the reality of my own experience of pain inflicted by Christians and of the pain I inflict on others. What am I to do with the problem of human evil when it directly affects my own life? I have theories. I have beliefs. Now am I going to assent to those beliefs? One author has described my dilemma this way: "Either one embraces the mystery of created freedom and accepts that the union of free spiritual creatures with the God of love is a thing so wonderful that the power of creation to enslave itself to death must be permitted by God; or one judges that not even such rational freedom is worth the risk of a cosmic fall and the terrible injustice of the consequences that follow from it."[4] It is neither piety to accept it nor liberation to reject it. But it is a choice I must make and then live out. My choice will affect how I process all future encounters with human selfishness, pride, envy, deceit, and a host of other evils. There is no triumphalism here, only heartbreak in knowing the beauty of humankind is marred, and we are the ones who have ripped ourselves apart.

• CONSIDERATIONS •

1. How has the pain and suffering in the world affected your view of God?
2. Do you think God is the answer to the problem of human suffering? Why or why not?
3. Why couldn't God just get rid of all the evil in the world right now?
4. Are people basically good? Why or why not?

---

4 David Bentley Hart, *The Doors of the Sea* (Grand Rapids: Eerdmans, 2005), 69. I am not in agreement with some of Hart's theology, but his book on the problem of evil put words to the pain in my soul.

CHAPTER 7

PRINCE OF PEACE OR POSER

> And if Christ has not been raised, then our preaching is in vain and your faith is in vain. We are even found to be misrepresenting God, because we testified about God that he raised Christ, whom he did not raise if it is true that the dead are not raised.
>
> —THE APOSTLE PAUL, 1 CORINTHIANS 15:14–15

> For we did not follow cleverly devised myths when we made known to you the power and coming of our Lord Jesus Christ, but we were eyewitnesses of his majesty.
>
> —THE APOSTLE PETER, 2 PETER 1:16

I sat in silence in an old church office, nervously thumbing through a pile of papers in my lap that con-stituted my debate notes. It was June 2009 in Dearborn, Michigan, and I was about to do my first debate. I'd never felt this uncomfortable or nervous before. *Did I remember to answer all those loose-end questions and rebuttals to my argument? I think there's one or two I couldn't get to in time. Oh, bother! There's always another thing I could've done to prepare. Why am I even doing this? What have I got to prove?*

The door behind me opened, and David Wood swaggered into the room, but I kept up my last-minute preparations.

"Are you ready to go? It's almost time to begin."

I looked up at him and said nothing.

David paused and considered my unusually quiet demeanor before speaking. "You know, Mary Jo, before Muhammad Ali's first fight, he was super nervous as well."

I turned back toward my notes, thinking, *Yeah, but Muhammad Ali wasn't in a room full of people who knew a whole lot more about his subject than he did.*

At my non-response, David continued. "He was so nervous that he wet his pants."

I suddenly looked up at David, who was stone-cold serious. *Where is he going with this story? Is he trying to pep-talk me?* I started to smile at the absurdity of the situation. I was a Portland, Oregon, girl who didn't use to care about religion and who, in my first thirty years of life, had met only one Muslim. Now here I was, about to debate a Muslim, surrounded by people I didn't know or barely knew, being coached by an ex-atheist sociopath. It was all crazy. *Why am I doing any of this? How did I let David and Nabeel talk me into this?*

"No matter what you're thinking right now, you're prepared," David said. "So let's go."

Still musing that the whole situation was ridiculous, I gathered my things, saying, "Thanks, coach," with playful sarcasm.

As we strode into the small church venue, I noticed it was a

little over half full. *Good. I can't face a packed house right now.*
After the introductions, I was up first. No problem, this first part
was basically reading an opening statement word-for-word. Then
the Muslim debater, Usaid, offered his own opening statement.
Originally, I had asked Usaid to debate on the **Christ myth theory** because he seemed to use the argument often. He declined,
so most of his opening remarks were on the historicity of Jesus's
death, as per our debate subject, "Did Jesus Die on the Cross?"

However, just as Usaid neared
the end of his opening statement,
he snuck in a little Christ myth theory. "As for pre-Christian gods . . .
the story of a god dying and rising
again is not unique to Christianity.
It's been done before. There's the
pagan god of Inanna who was crucified and was resurrected. And this is
a very old story, which was preserved
in clay tablets in 1500 BCE, starting
a very old tradition. And of course
there's Apollonius of Tyanna, which
I will get to later because I do not
have time."

I feverishly wrote notes and collected my rebuttals. After whirlwind
first rebuttals, I was able to address
the pagan myth claim in the second
rebuttal. "Now let me treat the pagan myths. If you're comparing
deities that never lived on earth, who have no historical narratives
placing their births or deaths during an era or in a place—and
who are not even a human—with Jesus, whom the Qu'ran affirms

Christ myth theory:
A belief that Jesus
was not an historical
person but rather his
story is a myth similar
to various other pagan
gods throughout time
(Osiris, Horus, Mithras,
etc.); also called the
pagan myth theory. If
Jesus did live, myth
theorists believe he did
not have anything to
do with the start of the
Christian faith in the
manner given by the
Gospel accounts.

as at least a human, then this is a huge problem for you. You're using an argument that goes against the Qu'ran. Further, many of the dying and rising gods such as Inanna and her substitution in the netherworld, Dumuzi, are tied to seasonal cycles of plant life. Dumuzi comes forth from the netherworld and Inanna goes down to the netherworld—they exchange places. This is not Jesus's story. T. N. D. Mettinger, one of the best scholars on ancient Near Eastern religions, says, 'Jesus' death is presented in the sources as a vicarious suffering, as an act of atonement for our sins, and is not comparable to any other dying and rising god.'

"There is no other dying and rising god that acts as a sacrifice, an atoning sacrifice for the sins of humankind. And finally with the pagan myths . . . the pagan myth theory could be equally applied with the same superficiality in order to refute the reliability of the Qur'an. For in the Qur'an we find a creation story that's similar to many preexisting pagan creation stories. We can find pagan practices in Islam. You have the circling of the Kaaba. If we were to look at all the ideas found in the Qur'an that predate Muhammad's report of the same ideas, we would be able to say that Muhammad used those same ideas in order to form his new religion of Islam. This is exactly what you are arguing against Christianity. This is very slippery ground, my friend."

I threw in one last punch as my time was ending: "And Apollonius of Tyana . . . you need to get rid of this. If you're going to accuse Christians of using late material for sources, you cannot use Apollonius of Tyana. His material dates to one hundred twenty-five years *after* Jesus's death. This is not a good source."

As Usaid began his second rebuttal he went directly after my retort, arguing that Christian apologists respond to accusations that Christianity has pagan roots simply by accusing Islam of pagan roots as well. *He missed my argument. It would be an error in reasoning (a* tuo quoque *fallacy) to say, "Oh yeah, well, Islam has pagan roots too. So there!"* If that were my only response, and I had not answered the objections laid against Christianity, then I would be guilty of the fallacy. But I did answer his accusations against Christianity's pagan roots. I was saying something quite different.

I'm arguing that if you're going to say that something preexisted Christianity and so therefore *it is the cause of Christianity*—which is what the copycat version of the Christ myth theory purports—then one could also apply that *line of reasoning* to Islam and discover the exact same problem. The argument he used would undercut the reliability of the Quranic text he is trying to support. This problem is partially due to the fact that the Christ myth argument, in this copycat form, is a post hoc argument (see below). Usaid needed to provide some direct evidence that Christians borrowed from earlier stories. Show the line of reasoning. Show the causation. Correlation does not imply causation.

I was first exposed to this copycat version of the Christ myth argument via my new blog. In those early years of my blog I would frequently check my analytics and discovered that many people were searching for "Osiris and Jesus" or "Horus and Jesus" when they found my blog. These results intrigued me, but I really became invested after I heard the copycat theory used by a Muslim debater in the Easter debates that David, Nabeel, and I put together. After Nabeel had answered an audience questioner on paganism and Christianity, saying that Christians did not borrow from pagan religions, one of the Muslim debaters responded:

> Alright, um, he's wrong. It's a *fact* that Christians did have a man-god [sic] like the pagans: there's Mithra, Osiris, Dionysis, and all these other pagan gods that were said to have been men to have died for the sins of the world or resurrected at

this time of the year. So Nabeel, come on, really; I think you need to check some history because you're totally wrong about that. It is documented that your practices are found in, uh, paganism, and are from paganism. The whole thing: Easter, the day you worship on, the beliefs that you have. Check it. Your beliefs are not original. Go look at Osiris, Mithra, and various other gods out there. Your belief that Jesus rose from the dead is not new. The pagans had that before you. Okay? Please check your history. And all you Christians, check it. Go look up encyclopedias and you'll see. Your beliefs are not new. There were many people who were said to be sons of God who died and rose on the third day. I'm telling you, check it.[1]

So that's exactly what I did. I checked it out. Only I went beyond the internet articles and the infamous internet film *Zeitgeist* that popularized this argument. I decided to trace this argument back to its roots, but first I wanted to uncover why this argument was so wildly popular today.

AN ARGUMENT RIDDLED WITH PROBLEMS

The copycat argument has been given quite the celebrity power boost at the start of the twenty-first century. Bill Maher, a political comedian, in a 2008 appearance on *The View*, stated in front of millions of viewers that the story of Jesus is "an exact copy of the story of Horus." A British celebrity, Stephen Fry, host of the television show *QI* (Quite Interesting), dedicated an entire program

---

1 Adapted statement by Shadid Lewis during the Easter debates at Central Baptist Church in Ghent, Virginia, 2008. Nabeel Qureshi and Sami Zaatari, "Who Was Jesus?" *YouTube* video, 3:09, July 22, 2008, 3:05:36–3:07:00, https://www.youtube.com/watch?v=tLbAi1Chkso.

to demonstrating that Christianity is a copy of the story of the Roman god, Mithras. The show, which aired during the Christmas season, was even titled, "Merry Mithras." Further, the best-selling author and atheist Richard Dawkins uses the catchy phrase, "We are all atheists about most of the gods that humanity has ever believed in. Some of us just go one god further."[2] He effectively lumps all the world's religious stories, as well as their theology and philosophy, into one simplistic category, as if there are no truly significant differences among any of them. Yet I can see why such a poorly constructed argument, riddled with the most basic of logical problems, perpetuates in the broader public. Our celebrity culture, which idolizes famous people, has become a platform for lots of dubious arguments. Pair that with the fact that most of us are no longer taught sound reasoning skills (logic), and you have confusion, fallacious reasoning, and deception. This scenario is exactly what's happening with this popular argument.

The copycat argument purports that because there are similarities between Jesus and earlier pagan stories, that the founders of Christianity, or at least the authors of the New Testament, borrowed the earlier stories to create

Post hoc ergo propter hoc: a Latin phrase that means "after this, therefore because of this."

Christianity. The first problem with this argument is that it commits an error in reasoning known as "after this, therefore because of this" fallacy, aka the *post hoc ergo propter hoc* fallacy. The argument assumes that because one story is later in time than

---

2 Richard Dawkins, "Militant Atheism," *TED*, YouTube video, February 2002, https://www.ted.com/talks/richard_dawkins_on_militant_atheism?language=en#t -499352. Cf. Richard Dawkins, *The God Delusion* (New York: Mariner, 2008), 77.

another story, and has some correlations, the later story is caused by the earlier stories.

Next, the arguer will show some vague similarities such as virgin birth, resurrection, salvation, death of the savior/hero, etcetera. However, as I began to look into these claimed similarities, I found that "virgin birth" could mean anything in the pagan stories from a woman who had previously been sexually active many times, to a goddess who scooped male sperm out of a lake, to the sexual intercourse of two god fetuses inside a goddess mother's womb, to a god who jumps out of the underworld via a rock near a river. These are the kind of "virgin births" that are considered to be the boilerplate for Jesus being born of a virgin. The arguer seems to have a broad and unhelpful definition for what constitutes a virgin birth.

For example, let's say I asked you if you wanted to go get a steak with me. You say, "That sounds amazing! I haven't had steak in so long." So we jump in my car and I drive you to the closest McDonald's restaurant. As we pull up, you question my restaurant choice, saying, "I thought we were going to get steak?" I respond with, "Yep, we are! They serve steak here." Of course, being a little confused, you say, "But that's not really steak, Mary Jo. You do understand that McDonald's makes burgers, right? That's quite different." What would you think if I said, "Nah, that's the same thing. Don't be ridiculous. McDonald's serves steak." You'd probably think I was a bit insane or just joking with you.

Now imagine that instead of a McDonald's, I pull up to a Chick-fil-A restaurant. You again question my decision. I respond with, "Yep, we're getting steak. They serve steak here." You say, "No, Mary Jo. Chicken is not the same thing as beef." If I responded with, "Well, they're both edible. It's the same thing," you'd think I was definitely messing with you or I had some seriously flawed beliefs.

If I pull up to an auto mechanic shop and say, "We're here to get our steak," your protest becomes more indignant as you try to explain the fundamental difference between an oil change and a steak dinner. I fire back with, "But oil nourishes cars and that's similar to how food nourishes humans." Vague similarities are not real correlations.

If a "birth" story is fundamentally different from a "virgin" birth, there's no honest way to say that those are the same things; *i.e., a god jumping out of a rock versus a female human who has never had sexual intercourse is not the same birth story.* So even though correlation doesn't imply causation, you'd at least want to have an *actual* correlation if you're going to argue that way. That's the poor reasoning in the copycat argument. It's really that bad, and yet it gets worse.

I said the argument was a post hoc argument, which is why you'd need evidence that the earlier stories were the actual source of the later Christian story. The arguer would need to show that it was more than just coincidence or more than similar matters producing similar lines of thinking.

One of the most famous examples of the problem of correlation and causation comes from the novel *Futility*. This novel is about an ocean liner whose owner, thinking the ship is unsinkable, sends it across the Atlantic with only the minimum required lifeboats. In the story, the gigantic ship hits an iceberg and sinks, killing most of its passengers and crew. While one might think this novel was inspired by the historical disaster of the *Titanic*, it was published fourteen years *before* the *Titanic* disaster. Author Morgan Robertson published the novel *Futility* in 1898. The *Titanic* sank in 1912.

The correlations between the two stories are uncanny: (1) both ships were considered unsinkable; (2) both hit icebergs in the month of April; (3) both hit the iceberg at around 22–25 knots; (4) the ships were 880 and 882 feet respectively; (5) both ship names are similar: the *Titan* and the *Titanic*; (6) both sank 400 miles off the coast of Newfoundland in the North Atlantic; (7) one ship had 2,200 passengers, and the other, 2,500 passengers; and (8) both ships carried the bare legal minimum of lifeboats.[3] By the reasoning used in the copycat theory, we'd have to acquiesce that the sinking of the *Titanic* was borrowed from the earlier story of the *Titan*, the implication being that therefore, the *Titanic* story is a false myth like the novel.

Although there is archaeological evidence and eyewitness testimony concerning the sinking of the *Titanic*—for comparison to the Christian story—what will that matter in two thousand years? It will not matter to the post hoc arguer, who could argue that the sinking of the *Titanic* is a myth because it correlates to an earlier existing story. The problem with a post hoc argument is that correlation isn't enough to prove causation. You have to definitively show that the earlier "this" caused the later "that."

Maybe you would protest, "But that's different, because we're talking about religion, not about an ocean liner and a novel. It's just not the same." Right. It's not the same; I'm using the same line of reasoning but in a different setting. I'm using the copycat argument but inserting different terms. If the argument is valid, it should still work unless we have any false premises. It doesn't work, though, because there is an error in reasoning involved. If the arguer used this kind of post hoc argument in other settings, they'd discover there are far-reaching implications.

Think of just one legal ramification. If you were at the scene of a gas station robbery before the robbery happened, you could

---

3 Heba Hasan, "Author 'Predicts' *Titanic* Sinking 14 Years Earlier," *Time* (April 14, 2012), http://newsfeed.time.com/2012/04/14/author-predicts-titanic-sinking-14-years -earlier/.

be convicted because your appearance at the scene of the crime must have been the cause of the crime. The correlation is your presence, and your presence proves you were the cause of the crime. Perhaps you were wearing a red sweatshirt and the robber was wearing a red sweatshirt, so obviously you were the robber. This scenario is quite a stretch, but it is born of the post hoc reasoning error. The prosecuting attorney cannot simply say, "Hey look, there's some correlation here . . . so obviously the defendant is guilty." That attorney has to at least establish motive, means, and opportunity to prove, beyond the shadow of a reasonable doubt, that you are guilty. With the copycat argument attorney, you're guilty based on the correlation alone.

EVEN DEEPER PROBLEMS

The copycat argument has other problems. It reduces Christianity to a straw man of its actual theological and philosophical positions in order to make it similar to the pagan stories, another error in reasoning. Philosopher Peter Kreeft describes that one of the benefits of learning logic is that logic can deduce the necessary consequences of a belief and therefore how that belief is applied to various life situations.[4] One of the most flagrant violations of logic in this argument is the lack of attention to this one giant detail: the pagan myths and Christianity have fundamental theological and philosophical differences that result in distinctly different ways of living for their adherents. Let's look at just one.

In 1 Corinthians 15, Paul describes the reality of the resurrection of Jesus to be a life-altering event for anyone who believes it

---

4 Peter Kreeft, *Socratic Logic: A Logic Text Using Socratic Method, Platonic Questions, and Aristotelian Principles* (South Bend, IN: St. Augustine's, 2010), 4.

really happened. He does so by arguing from contrasting beliefs. He says in verses 14–15 that if Christ hasn't risen from the dead, then Christian faith is in vain and so is its preaching. He also notes that Christians would be giving false testimony about God. Further, in verse 19, he says that if hope in Christ is true only for this life, then Christians are to be pitied among all men. Paul argues that there is a way one should live and act if indeed Christ has risen from the dead. He does so by way of contrast, declaring that if there is no resurrection, we should "eat and drink, for tomorrow we die" (v. 32). The implication is that a person's view of God affects their philosophy of life, and in turn, their actions, habits, and culture.

Paul closes out his writing in this section by noting that the influence of the surrounding culture is corrupting the Corinthian believers, when, in verse 33, he quotes the Greek poet Menander, "Bad company corrupts good character." Notice that Paul is strongly implying that distinctive choices and lifestyles will result from a person's beliefs. Christians believe they will be resurrected like Christ (1 Corinthians 15:20). Therefore, they are not to cling to earthly wealth, pleasures, or even their own lives. They are to graciously give of themselves to others, as they have received the ultimate grace from God. This theology has been demonstrated for two thousand years in the sacrifices of Christians in service to their communities and to the world.

However, pagans didn't have a resurrected savior who vicariously atoned for their evil. Nor did pagans know what would happen to them in the afterlife. They didn't know if their soul would be annihilated, imprisoned in Hades, or blissfully released to reside in the land of the gods. However, they did believe that they would be released from their physical bodies for all eternity, and this belief greatly impacted their lives. The early church father, Ambrose, bishop of Milan, noted,

If all hope of the resurrection is lost, let us eat and drink and lose not the enjoyment of the things present, for we have none to come. . . . The Epicureans say they are followers of pleasure because death means nothing to them, because that which is dissolved has no feeling, and that which has no feeling means nothing to us. Thus they show that they are living only carnally, not spiritually. They do not discharge the duty of the soul but only of the flesh. They think that all life's duty is ended with the separation of the soul and body.[5]

These are very different views of the nature of reality and the nature of the afterlife—and we've not even begun to scratch the surface on this matter! Ambrose described that the philosophy of the pagan works out into pagan lives much differently than how Christian beliefs work in the lives of Christians. The pagans were much more focused on the present life and the pleasures of it. The copycat argument ignores this massive difference altogether in making its case. If Christians had borrowed from pagan theology, they seemed to have missed the major philosophical underpinnings of the pagan beliefs. Rather, my conclusion was the same as scholar Larry Hurtado's in *One God, One Lord: Early Christian Devotion and Ancient Jewish Monotheism*: "Early Christian devotion did not result from a clumsy crossbreeding of Jewish monotheism and pagan polytheism under the influence of gentile Christians too ill-informed about the Jewish heritage to preserve its character."[6]

Maybe I need to throw this argument back on the arguers and ask, "Why does this story exist at all? As you've shown, there

5   Gerald Bray, ed., *Ancient Christian Commentary New Testament Volume VII: 1 & 2 Corinthians* (Downers Grove, IL: InterVarsity Press, 1999), 167.

6   Larry Hurtado, *One God, One Lord: Early Christian Devotion and Ancient Jewish Monotheism* (New York: Continuum, 1998), 100.

are similarities to it in stories everywhere throughout time and history." C. S. Lewis wrote on this matter that one great general story has indeed been told in many forms over the years. He sees this one great story as reflective of the human metanarrative, the narrative of salvation history, even with all its subsequent twisting and perversions. His view, in a way, treats all these stories as different theories on reality, with the Christian theory having the most plausibility. It's like my dad used to say: "If you have three engineers working on one problem, you'll have four hypotheses." To which I'd respond, "But one of them is the closest to truth."

MORE LESSONS LEARNED

I came away from my first debate with two main thoughts: (1) a confirmation of the copycat argument as a bad argument and (2) a realization that inattention to the logic involved in the argumentation can cause further problems. I don't think Usaid understood that his own line of reasoning as a Muslim debater could be used against his Muslim beliefs. His use of poor arguments against belief in the Christian God led to poor reasoning about God in general, and that is not a problem specific to this debater. Rather, I find this problem to be common among us humans. *In fact, I wonder how many people have stepped away from the faith because of poorly reasoned and poorly evidenced arguments?* Further, it is quite difficult to avoid poor reasoning, especially when we haven't had any training in how to think well.

The debate taught me through real-life experience the importance of orderly thinking. It showed me the usefulness of being able to clearly organize my thoughts on a matter and then to see how those thoughts relate to each other. *What conclusions result from those thoughts in a commonsense way (what conclusions logically flow from the premises)? Or am I getting to conclusions without the support needed to get me there?* As I studied for the debate, I began to see deficiencies not only in my opponent's views but also in my own arguments for God. Some of my thoughts didn't add up to my conclusions "naturally." I was holding some beliefs without having ever thought seriously on them or having tried to justify them. These deficiencies became clearer as I increasingly engaged with those who opposed my views. I saw how a person can become pigeonholed in their thinking by not having their thoughts and presuppositions challenged, or by not entertaining serious thought on the opposing viewpoint. As Proverbs explains, "The one who states his case first seems right, until the other comes and examines him" (Proverbs 18:17). I wondered how many times I had jumped to a conclusion on an issue before reflecting on it in a serious way.

Many times, in church ministry, Roger and I have been on the receiving end of a poorly constructed argument that seemed rash and emotive rather than carefully investigated. The more I understood my lack of training in logical argumentation, the more I began to see a lack of training in logic and reasoned argumentation within the broader body of Christ. Most of the arguments levied against Roger or me were not well constructed and couldn't stand up to rigorous scrutiny. If I investigated a person's main points, I was often met with defensive posturing, self-assured arrogance, or even a hyperspiritualizing of the situation. *But what was I to do?* It is one thing to recognize a problem in the church and quite another to address it. Yet that is exactly what I decided to do. Instead of merely lodging complaints, I decided to help Christians develop better reasoning skills by teaching classes on "Recognizing Bad Reasoning." I don't know how much difference it has made, but I really wish more churches and Christian colleges would teach good reasoning skills.

Debating opened my eyes to the fact that people don't generally argue well, nor care to do so. Sometimes Christians give God a bad reputation from a lack of serious attention to the forming of the mind. I could see how some of the hurt that I'd experienced in church came from a lack of good argumentation, and even sometimes just from straight-up arrogance. While we aren't all going to have the same capabilities or capacities to argue well, we should never use a lack of reasoning as an excuse for belligerence. And conversely, if we do argue well but with a spirit of arrogance or spite, we are in serious need of spiritual formation and discipline. Once I realized that we all need help in these areas, I realized also that my own unrealistic expectations of people intensified my angst with the church.

• CONSIDERATIONS •

1. What does the copycat version of the pagan myth theory say about the story of Jesus?
2. Why is the copycat argument a poor argument against Christianity?
3. How does good or bad reasoning affect your view of God?
4. How does the ability to argue well affect our relationships with fellow Christians?

CHAPTER 8

A CONCERNING VOID

It is easier to hide behind philosophical arguments,
heavily footnoted for effect, than it is to admit our hurts,
our confusions, our loves, and our passions in the
marketplace of life's heartfelt transactions.

—RAVI ZACHARIAS, *CAN MAN LIVE WITHOUT GOD*

Nothing is good enough for me. I am painfully aware that I always could have done something better and feel like I'm always missing out on something in life. I constantly seem to crave that one more thing that will make me happy, satisfied, or fulfilled. Yet the more things I get or accomplishments I make, the more my heart seeks that elusive "one thing more." At times my yearnings have made me push myself beyond my physical and mental capabilities. In addition, my desire to fulfill my longings has affected those closest to me. One annual event that highlights this issue is my birthday.

"Hey, JoJo, whatcha want to do for your birthday?" Roger asked one year.

"Oh, you want *me* to choose a place to go for my birthday?"

"Yeah, we can go anywhere you like."

"I thought you'd just pick a place and take me there. You know, kind of like a surprise?"

Roger furrowed his brows a little. "I thought about that, but the last couple of times I did that, you weren't happy with where we went. So, instead, I decided to take you wherever you want to go. I obviously don't make good choices."

Anger welled up in my stomach. Roger was using a cop-out to get out of the work of planning a great birthday for me. Yet I always decorated and spent a considerable amount of time finding great gifts for his and Emily's birthdays. It felt as though he was giving up on me before he even started. So I pushed back a little.

"How come I always seem to find something you guys like, but when it comes to me you don't seem to spend as much time figuring out what I like?"

Roger didn't answer me right away. He had an agonized look on his face as though he was trying to not say what he wanted to say. Finally, he looked me straight in the eye and said, "You are never happy with any situation. You will always find something wrong with it. So that makes it hard to find somewhere to go or something to do that will make you happy. For instance, at a restaurant, you'll be upset that the waiters aren't paying enough attention to us, or that the room is too loud, or the music is too loud, or the food isn't up to your expectations. Plus, you are always wondering if it would have been better to go somewhere else."

My anger began to boil. Not only was I disappointed in how I was being treated on my birthday, but the truth of Roger's words churned like a hot acid in my stomach. *He's right and you know it*. I remained silent.

"Remember that turquoise bracelet and ring I got you when we were younger? You almost never wore them. When you opened the gift, you were obviously disappointed. I realized at that moment that I had no idea what you liked. However, I have come to realize that you don't seem to know either."

"Okay, okay . . . I get it. I'm difficult to impress."

"Jo, you're not difficult, you're nearly *impossible* to impress, which makes me not even want to try. I know that every time I'm going to get it wrong. As a result, I leave it up to you to figure out."

There it was. Out came the searing truth that has slowly burned in our marriage for years . . . I'm nearly impossible to impress. *How awful it must be for Roger to be married to a girl he feels he can never impress!* I had always prided myself on going the extra mile and being the best in whatever I do. Now I was finding my perfectionist attitude had greatly hurt my relationship with Roger.

One could say that my discontentment in birthday celebrations mirrored the broader problem I had with church community: my expectations created a reality in which nothing was ever good enough for me. Walking into the church my first day as a Christian, I brought along my perfectionism and unrealistic expectations of what I thought should happen. Surely these were the people who truly sought God, had been transformed by their beliefs, and constantly demonstrated that transformation. They were the pros! I could learn from them and grow into the Christian I envisioned I could be! When I discovered that people in the church were just regular people, with all the same problems as any other group of humans, I was bitterly disappointed.

For several years, I fantasized that somewhere on this planet there was a perfectly healthy church with perfectly healthy leadership. Of course, I hadn't taken the time to define "healthy," but if I'm brutally honest, I probably thought "healthy" meant people who were more like me. I lamented for the church I had imagined from reading the Bible, never recalling that the earliest followers of Christ, as chronicled by New Testament authors, struggled with their own hypocrisy, doubt, selfishness, argumentativeness, belligerence, lust, and greed. What I hoped to find among Christians on this earth has been a struggle for the church since its start. Yet this attitude of perfectionism which made me quite critical of the Christian faith also made me critical of atheism.

ARGUMENTS AND EXPECTATIONS

When I decided to explore the arguments for atheism, I think I unrealistically expected the arguments to be smarter, sleeker, sexier. I also expected atheists to be more thoughtful, less authoritarian, and generally more relaxed in attitude. *I mean, what do they have to prove?* Rather, the atheist evangelists I encountered, specifically online, were haughty, arrogant, and belligerently dogmatic in their beliefs. Instead of actually arguing about the evidence, these people were more interested in making me look foolish or stupid, while conversely making themselves appear thoughtful, studied, and sure. Their engagements with me were laced with negatively charged wording and caricatures of Christianity. Here are some examples from my online debate forum and my blog:

- "Those beliefs of hers are to be described simply as bizzaro! If she understood the full range of problems for the Christian faith, then she would never have believed in the first place!"

- "Ultimately faith does not require evidence, or it would not be faith."
- "FYI: The only solution to the problem of evil is that your god is incompetent, weak, evil, or fiction. Why do you worship that?"
- "In my opinion it's okay to hate people who shield their bigotry behind a Bronze Age book of fables."[1]
- "There are two approaches to faith: blind faith without thought and the intellectual one which makes impossible excuses for implausible ideas."

It felt like I was being held accountable for someone else's poor behavior, perhaps some nineteenth-century, hellfire-and-brimstone preacher railing against atheists. Even though my goal in hosting a debate forum was to openly engage ideas, very few interactions were cordial, winsome, or devoid of personal attacks, nor did my opponents appear to be genuinely interested in thinking through the evidence.[2] In making arguments online, I bemoaned to Roger that I often had to play "mom," chiding others for name-calling. Still, even with all the name-calling, I was willing to engage arguments if any would be made.

These interactions profoundly impacted my predicament with the Christian church, which is why I bring it up at all. I gained firsthand experience that these atheist followers of the vast, indifferent universe, who claimed intellectual and moral superiority, were not effectively demonstrating such claims. Why were atheists, who professed to be liberated and free, acting no

---

better than the hurtful people I encountered in the church? If their thinking was so much clearer after having been brought out from under the spell of religion, then where was the evidence of how much better human beings they had become? Rather, I noticed that I found the same problems within the atheist community as I did within the Christian community: judgmentalism, superficiality, arrogance. Still, as with Christianity, I couldn't grant the abuse of a philosophy as the litmus test for the truth or falsity of that system of thought.

Therefore, I began to study the atheist claims in greater depth. I realized that, as much as I didn't like the behaviors I found on both sides of the debate, I could at least deduce that the Christians who were hurtful *were* being hypocrites in accordance with their views. The apostle Paul admonishes the attitude and behavior problems in the church when he addresses the Jewish law with believers in Rome:

> You then who teach others, do you not teach yourself? You who preach against stealing, do you steal? You who say that people should not commit adultery, do you commit adultery? You who abhor idols, do you rob temples? You who boast in the law, do you dishonor God by breaking the law? As it is written: "God's name is blasphemed among the Gentiles because of you." (Romans 2:21–24 NIV)

Grounding: Something is said to "ground" another thing if it accounts for the being/ existence of the second thing—the conditions for something to come into existence.

Paul directly links hypocrisy in the church to the Gentile's rejection of God. His admonishment here assumes that a moral standard is not only real but discoverable within the

Christian worldview and that believers should be held accountable for adhering to it. So hypocrisy is a real problem for the Christian. I could not say the same for the atheist. One must have an objective standard before one can break it. The underlying assumption in Christianity is that the ground for the moral standard is found in God's nature, his perfect goodness. As far as I could tell, atheists had no such standard, or at least no way of **grounding** one outside of themselves.

A famous Carl Sagan quote exemplifies the problem for the atheistic view: "The Cosmos is all that is or was or ever will be."[3] Sagan expounds that the material universe is all that exists (the foundation of materialistic thinking). If all that exists is matter, then an **objective** moral standard, being an immaterial concept, cannot find a home in a strictly material universe. Hypocrisy requires a reference to a standard of moral conduct which a person verbally accepts, but then denies by their behavior. The concept of hypocrisy is robbed of meaning in a materialistic understanding of the universe.

Though Christianity failed to meet my expectations, it was because my expectations were unrealistic for the reality of the situation. Now I faced the atheist worldview and found my expectations were unmet, not because they were unrealistic but exactly because those expectations *were realistic*. I say this all the while

Objective: To be "independent of people's (including one's own) opinion." Its opposing term, *subjective*, means "just a matter of personal opinion."

Adapted from William Lane Craig, "Question of the Week #347: 'Objective' or 'Absolute' Moral Values?," Reasonable Faith, www.reasonablefaith.org/writings/question-answer/objective-or-absolute-moral-values/.

---

3 Carl Sagan, *Cosmos* (New York: Ballantine, 1980), 337.

recognizing my desire to be liberated from the pain of living in church community. *If only atheism were true, all this conflict and strife with the church would be moot.* Yet the deeper I dove into atheist views, the larger gaps I found, gaps I simply could not take a blind leap to overcome. Two of the large flaws I discovered in the atheistic system were (1) the failure to address the internal needs of humanity and (2) the failure to demonstrate reasoning as trustworthy.

THE FAILURE TO ADDRESS THE INTERNAL NEEDS OF HUMANITY

Human beings have a basic internal need to establish meaning, purpose, and value.[4] One of the means by which we establish these things is through the guidance of a moral compass: determining what is good and what is not good. One of the most frequently quoted authors to me in my early years of doubt was the popular atheist professor of Oxford University, Richard Dawkins. He is an evolutionary biologist with a charming British accent who has a personal vendetta against religion. He has this to say about finding our way in the universe:

> In a universe of blind physical forces and genetic replication, some people are going to get hurt, other people are going to get lucky, and you won't find any rhyme or reason in it, nor any justice. The universe we observe has precisely the properties we should expect if there is, at bottom, no design, no

---

4 The arguments briefly touched upon here date back thousands of years, with great amounts of work having been done in the last two thousand years. I in no way intend to attempt a proof of my view in such a limited space. Rather, I hope you can get a glimpse of my thinking on these matters.

purpose, no evil, no good, nothing but blind, pitiless indifference. . . . DNA neither knows nor cares. DNA just is. And we dance to its music.[5]

Within a materialist framework, there is, at bottom, nothing upon which to build a moral compass or law. The universe lacks such intentionality. As Dawkins describes, he not only believes this view to be so, but he *sees a universe* that has no moral qualities. I find his statement to be rather obtuse.

Even as a person who didn't believe in God, I saw moral qualities to the universe, such as things that are good and things that are bad (e.g., loving my mom versus hating my mom). More so, I couldn't get around the moral qualities, as it is frustratingly difficult to do so.[6] A quick glance at Dawkins's own statement of belief in a non-moral universe utilizes the word *hurt* set against the word *unlucky*. Doesn't *hurt* imply something is wrong? Doesn't *unlucky* contrast a favorable *lucky*, which would imply that one is good and the other is bad? You are not "hurt" or functioning improperly if there is no way that things are supposed to be, if there is no standard by which to judge something as wrong. It is not "better" to have random chance go one way or the other, so lucky and unlucky are actually meaningless colloquialisms.

Embedded in the language Dawkins uses are concepts that reveal a belief in something as a standard of the way things should be—a standard of goodness—while denying there is such a standard. Certainly, it's possible to make such assertions as "there is

5   Richard Dawkins, *River Out of Eden: A Darwinian View of Life* (New York: Basic Books, 1995), 133.

6   Even just a cursory look at the handling of the Moral Law arguments proposed and rebutted over the centuries will demonstrate the difficulty in waving off a morally charged universe.

no standard of goodness," but such assertions are unlivable for humans. Even when we attempt to argue against moral qualities, we use language that is given meaning by a standard of goodness, which leaves a lot to be explained if the universe has no moral qualities.

Of course, some atheist thinkers will argue that objective moral values can be explained by the evolutionary process of natural selection. As author Kenneth Samples conveys,

> Some naturalists have even suggested that human belief in such things as God, immortality, and objective moral values was produced in man as a means of promoting human survivability. So even though these ideas (e.g., god) are actually false, they somehow supported man's ability to survive and even thrive. But this theory would mean that false beliefs may at times do more to promote human flourishing than true beliefs.[7]

The problem with this argumentation, as noted by Samples, is that it leads one to the inescapable consequence that natural selection could just as easily produce false beliefs as it could produce true beliefs. The goal of natural selection is survival, not truth. One could never know if one's beliefs were true, false, or a survival mechanism. We couldn't trust our reasoning faculties to produce truth. Therefore, we couldn't trust the moral values we gained through natural selection as being true or right.

If, as Dawkins noted, I am just dancing to the music of my DNA, then everything I think and do is determined by the arrangement of my atoms. An arrangement of atoms is not

---

7   Kenneth Samples, *A World of Difference: Putting Christian Truth Claims to the Worldview Test* (Grand Rapids: Baker, 2007), 212.

charged with moral implications; it just is. Rather than choice and consequence, we are dealing with cause and effect. For instance, I cannot say that loving my mother is good; it really is just my DNA doing what it does. There is no real moral value to loving her. Therefore, there is no real moral value to hating her, as well. I have no realistic means of making sense of the morally charged world in which I seem to live.

Further, since everything I do is predetermined, there is no choice in the matter. Without real choice, there is no real consequence. How would you make sense of a concept like consequence when there is no choice involved? Rather, it would be cause and effect, a non-morally charged situation. If I love my mother, it wasn't my choice and so there is no consequently *appropriate* response to my love. My love just is. It is not morally praiseworthy, just as my hatred of my mother would not be morally blameworthy. If I were to get drunk and drive, hitting another vehicle and killing the passengers, the result would be a matter of cause and effect, not choice and consequence. Again, my actions would not be morally blameworthy. Society may have agreements (laws) so that they can live in community with each other, but there is no grounded reason to see an ill in this situation.

I attempted to communicate my struggle with this conundrum in a conversation with a few atheists online. My thoughts on the matter were still so new that I didn't always express myself very well. So in attempting a clarification with one gentleman, I said:

> If I were to murder you or a beloved just for kicks, I think you would find it hard pressed to dismiss it as merely the way things are. You would intuitively understand this to in some way be a wrong action, and not just as defined by government, but as inherently wrong. However, in a universe devoid of a

transcendent standard of good, things such as rape, murder, and suffering are still ultimately brute facts, no meaning, no ethics involved. Just like you find God hard to accept due to the existence of evil, I find God hard to deny due to the existence of moral law.

In denying the existence of God, the problem of evil is still with us, so now what? Is it better explained? We humans would be the root of all problems and we do not appear to be getting better (or seem to know how to). And the natural disasters, well, that's just the way it is. There is no meaning, no lessons, and no "good" to come of anything, because there is no real "good" outside of human constructs. The universe is devoid of good. And it appears not to matter how much education, money, or help people get; there is still so much meaningless pain and suffering.

Some people I converse with seem to think humans will get or are getting morally better (I would disagree). But then, how long should we wait? Past our own deaths? And who is to judge me or you according to their view of right and wrong . . . a mere human? Who is able?

In response, I received this retort:

I think this means that Mary [Jo] considers herself above American law, as she does not think her fellow human beings in America are able to judge whether it is right or wrong for her to take crack cocaine.

I'm sure she doesn't take crack cocaine, but if she did, she would find her confident assertions about the inability of me to judge her to be somewhat reality-challenged. How can somebody write that human beings are not able to judge each other? I find such statements just plain weird. How can anybody become a Christian if it means saying in public that they do think "a mere human" can judge each other according to their view of right and wrong? Did her God create the speeding laws that she obeys? Did her God create the taxes that she pays? Humans created all those laws that Mary Jo obeys because she knows she will be judged as a criminal if she disobeys them. And human beings created all the laws in the Bible. . . . None of them were created by her alleged god.

This kind of response does not satisfy me. *Do people really think that grounding morality is this easy? Do they think that declaring their beliefs with an edgy tone of superiority makes their beliefs true?* His response merely described the way things are: that humans have developed laws by which they judge one another. However, I was asking for the *foundation* of those laws. Why think these laws match reality at all? I wanted explanations that were more intellectually and existentially satisfying if I was going to commit my life to certain beliefs.

With a lack of real choice and consequence, I fall into the further problem of meaning in human life. We as humans have the unique capacity to reflect on our own existence: *What is the meaning of life? Do I have purpose? Is this all there is to life and then I die?* Without true choice and consequence, my life is merely a pinball in the universe. I am bouncing around causing and effecting but not intending and purposing. Without any real intention or purpose, it is hard to ground meaning to what I do and who I am. There is no meaning behind random chance. Although humans can beautifully state what our lives mean to us, personal meaning and objective meaning are different. A child can make up a gibberish language that has meaning to her, but it doesn't have ultimate meaning outside the child's mind. I wanted meaning that transcended me. All atheism could tell me was that we should be true to ourselves. But without a way to ground these ideas, they are truly void of meaning. It's all just delusional.

Author Ravi Zacharias says,

> Outside of Christ there is no law, no hope, and no meaning. You, and you alone, are the determiner and definer of these essentials of life; you, and you alone, are the architect of your own moral law; you, and you alone, craft meaning for your own life; you, and you alone, risk everything you have on the basis of a hope you envisage. As a cynic once put it, "We are all in this together, alone." You have made life's greatest decision, taken the greatest gamble, and answered the greatest question of our time—if you choose to live without God.[8]

I've encountered pushback on this position. "Of course, humans can have meaning and purpose to their lives apart from God! Don't be ridiculous." Notice the subtle difference in the nuanced phrasing. Yes, humans *can have* meaning and purpose, but they cannot *have a grounding* for meaning and purpose.[9] Without a grounding, meaning and purpose are, at best, subjective to every individual with no corresponding objectivity, or, at worst, may be irresponsible wishful thinking. *This kind of*

---

8   Ravi Zacharias, *Can Man Live Without God* (Nashville: Thomas Nelson, 1994), 61, Kindle.
9   Friedrich Nietzsche believed we created our own values and meaning and purpose. He denied that these things had any substantive grounding other than what humans create. So there is no external reality to which our thoughts of value, meaning, and purpose match. There's no way to verify whether any of our thoughts on these matters are truthful or real.

reasoning simply isn't good enough for me. It does not demonstrate why humans are accountable to treat each other with even the base-level dignity of just allowing a human to have life.

People around the world risk their own lives and brutally end others' lives for what they believe is true about reality. Willingness to die or kill for one's beliefs isn't a phenomenon confined to religious believers. Atheistic-inspired leaders of the twentieth century have led some of the bloodiest campaigns in all human history, from Adolf Hitler to Joseph Stalin to Mao Zedong. Modern atheistic mythology claims that religions have been the cause of most wars, so if we can just progress beyond our religious beliefs, we'd finally learn to respect and love each other. However, statistics from the *Encyclopedia of Wars* show that conflicts categorized as "religious" come in at a low 7 percent.[10]

While this statistic doesn't show that religion was a complete nonfactor, it does show that it wasn't the primary motivator for most wars (although it may have been a means to justify a political end). As the fictional character, Ricky Ricardo, once

---

10 I originally encountered this statistic in Andy Bannister, *The Atheist Who Didn't Exist* (Oxford, England: Monarch, 2015), 106. Cf. Rabbi Alan Lurie, "Is Religion the Cause of Most Wars?" *Huffpost* (April 10, 2012), https://www.huffingtonpost.com/rabbi-alan-lurie/is-religion-the-cause-of-_b_1400766.html. Lurie expounds, "In their recently published book, 'Encyclopedia of Wars,' authors Charles Phillips and Alan Axelrod document the history of recorded warfare, and from their list of 1,763 wars only 123 have been classified to involve a religious cause, accounting for less than 7 percent of all wars and less than 2 percent of all people killed in warfare. While, for example, it is estimated that approximately one to three million people were tragically killed in the Crusades, and perhaps 3,000 in the Inquisition, nearly 35 million soldiers and civilians died in the senseless, and secular, slaughter of World War I alone. . . . Similarly, the vast numbers of genocides (those killed in ethic [sic] cleanses, purges, etc. that are not connected to a declared war) are not based on religion. It's estimated that over 160 million civilians were killed in genocides in the 20th century alone, with nearly 100 million killed by the Communist states of USSR and China."

said, "Lucy, you've got some 'splaining to do!" *Where is this brave new world that was supposed to emerge as the human race became less religious?* It has failed, in part, because the atheist view lacks explanatory power and existential force in meeting the basic internal human needs of meaning, purpose, and value.

THE FAILURE TO DEMONSTRATE HUMAN REASONING AS TRUSTWORTHY

During the exchange that followed my review of David's debate on the problem of evil, the atheist debater made this assertion: "Christians retreat, or punt, to background beliefs to help settle the problem of evil without which they would not believe in the first place. I mean really, if you looked at this present world and were asked whether or not an omni-God created it without reference to any other background belief of yours, I dare say you would conclude as I do."

I replied, "My background beliefs are atheist, so I'm uncertain as to what you mean by my background beliefs."

"Your background blinds you to the ability to see the truth of the matter."

"Again, I know my name is Mary Jo, which sounds very Southern-evangelical-Bible-Belt, and I do indeed live in the Bible Belt now, but I wasn't raised Christian. I'm also from a relatively non-Christian part of the United States. Regarding my background beliefs and education, nearly all of it was void of overt Christian influence. The things that were Christian influenced, I wouldn't have recognized as such on my own, having never been taught to do so . . . save perhaps the Christmas and Easter holidays." *I can't believe how many times my name and location have been a determining factor in another person's view of me.*

"Okay, you weren't Christian, but you are now. And there are assumptions in the background of your mind that allow you to accept things you'd never accept if those thoughts weren't there already."

"While I won't completely dismiss the idea that there are background influencers in my mind, I also won't completely dismiss the idea that I am capable of discovering truth even with the presence of those influencers. It's a difficult task, but possible. For instance, one of the reasons that I turned back to Christianity after doubting my faith was because of the discoverability of truth. I realized I trusted that human reasoning can function in a manner as to discover truth. However, when I looked at both atheism and Christianity as a source for that claim, I only found it to be the case within a Christian philosophical framework. Atheism, lacking its own source for trusting human reasoning, couldn't assure me that I was even on the right path to discovering truth."

"I never said you weren't capable of discovering truth."

"Thank you. I appreciate that. You did seem to suggest that I couldn't see the truth of the problem of evil because of my Christian background. But I don't want to leave out an important assertion: I am saying that atheism isn't a reliable system for discovering truth, due to its inability to ground trust in human reasoning."

"That's a ridiculous assertion. I'm just as capable as anyone else of discovering truth. You see what I mean about your background assumptions that keep you from understanding things?"

"Okay, let me explain."

One of the growing concerns I had with atheism was that the source of a human's rationality was not a rational source, nor a personal source, nor a purposive source. Rather, reason was the result of a "nonrational and impersonal process without purpose consisting of a combination of genetic mutation, variation, and environmental factors (natural selection)."[11] In other words, completely random chance was at the source of our complex human minds.

Yes, exactly. Humans are the product of blind, impersonal forces. What's the big deal? Well, that might seem to be a useful statement when trying to argue directly in opposition to Christianity and belief in God. But how useful is this statement when reflecting on one's own reasoning abilities? If nonrational sources produced my rationality, then why should I trust it? Remember back to our discussion on evolutionary morality: natural selection cannot give me truth. It only ensures survival. So, just as in the moral landscape, I cannot trust these blind, impersonal forces to produce reliable truth-making faculties, like rationality. This again, is the grounding problem.

From an atheistic perspective, natural selection produced belief in God because that belief aided in survival. Atheists also trust that this belief in God is false. So what conclusion can be drawn here . . . that evolutionary processes produce false beliefs? This conclusion undercuts all rational thinking. *What then, shall I suppose, is safe from my own flawed rationality? Perhaps I have no true beliefs whatsoever.*

Further, if atheism entails rationality arising from such an unreliable truth-making process, how can one know that atheism isn't just another one of the false beliefs? The riddles of atheism left me without an answer. Meanwhile, Christianity claims that the origin of the universe is a personal intelligence. This view states that rationality comes forth from rationality. It also states

11 Kenneth Samples, *A World of Difference: Putting Christian Truth Claims to the Worldview Test* (Grand Rapids: Baker, 2007), 211.

that our rationality came from a person with a will, meaning rationality serves a purpose. It is not a blind, impersonal process. *What would be the purpose of giving humans rationality?* To give humans reasoning abilities would seem to be so that we can know truth, but only if the rationality given is able and purposed toward the end of truth making. This is an argument that can be firmly argued within the Christian framework. It is also an argument that quickly loses ground in the atheist framework.

Considering that atheism fails to adequately address internal needs of humanity and fails to demonstrate human reasoning as trustworthy, I found too much lacking in the atheist view of the universe to accept it. As with the Dacey-Craig debate (found in chapter 3), the atheist shrugs his shoulders and says, "We just don't know." While I agree that there is a lot we don't know and there is much we think we know that we'll eventually see as wrong, there is too much surrendered here to justify how we know anything at all. The self-destruct mechanism is in the foundation of an atheistic worldview.

WHAT NEXT?

So there it was, the resultant conclusion: the thing that makes the most sense of the internal needs of humanity and of human reasoning as trustworthy is the existence of God. I suppose I should have done a happy dance and gleefully expressed my belief in God. Only that wasn't what happened. I felt rather lost. I didn't feel any sense of belonging in the Christian church, and my hope for atheism was shattered on its own foundations. Furthering my sense of isolation were the attacks I received from adherents to both viewpoints.

I remember Roger asking me one day why I seemed so downtrodden. I replied, "It's because I'm a Treebeard."

162 • WHY I STILL BELIEVE

"What?" Roger gently laughed. "What does that mean?"

"It means that I'm on nobody's side because nobody is on my side."[12]

As usual, Roger patiently waited for the rest of my explanation. "I haven't found what I'm looking for," I said. "I'm utterly disappointed. I thought I found the best thing ever when I found Christianity. Perhaps that's true. But when I went looking for Christianity on earth, I didn't really find it. I don't just want to fit in with church culture in any given geographic area. I want to be a part of a community that loves deeply and unconditionally, a community that values an individual in the beauty and mess of their individuality. And a community with ideas that are logically coherent. Where is that? Where?"

Roger looked at me solemnly. "What are you going to do?"

"I don't know. I'm tired of the shallowness of the people who say they believe in God. Neither am I impressed with the New Atheists. So what does that say about me?" I paused since I didn't know the answer. "I can't find a reasonable way around God's existence. Sure, I could begin to solely focus on the atheist arguments and try to buttress just that side of the debate. But in the back of my mind would be the annoying thought: *You don't believe this is true.*"

"Jo, I have an idea. You've been trying so hard to have this discussion with people in our own church. That's where the bulk of your angst is coming from. I think it's time to move your ministry entirely outside of our church. Go discuss these things with people who want to discuss them with you. Stop trying to

---

12 Treebeard is a character in J. R. R. Tolkien's *The Lord of the Rings* epic fantasy novel.

convince people who have no interest in these matters. Go serve God where he uses you."

And so I did. I recognized the rejection of my local church leadership and moved on. I had never tried to force anything on the church. I had never challenged any of the leaders publicly. The only time I spoke up was when a leader spread rumors that since I was doing a scientific apologetics class surveying all views of the relationship of science and faith, that I wasn't teaching the Bible as God's Word. Even at that, I met with him privately, discussed the accusation, and then asked him to apologize to anyone with whom he had shared that sentiment. He did so. But the damage was done. I was implicitly rejected from the church, which created quite an odd situation, since I was the worship minister's wife. Over the years that followed, people would ask me why I wasn't teaching apologetics at my home church. I never told them about the attack and the subsequent marginalization. I just moved on, although harboring distrust in my heart.

An atheist debater once wrote to me:

My own loss of faith was really just a failure to continue trusting men. "God" remains an open question, with the Christians who claim to know Him having failed spectacularly to agree on a coherent, consistent, credible version of their faith.

I had difficulty trusting people as well. But my lack of trust was more holistic, for I didn't trust people on either side of the debate. Chalk it up to my unrealistic expectations, or my perfectionism, or whatever you want to call it, but I was inconsolable. I felt like I had lost so much by becoming involved with Christians. It caused me to reflect on why I had gotten involved with the church at all. What was it that drew me to God?

CONSIDERATIONS

1. Why does hypocrisy make sense as a problem in a Christian worldview but not necessarily in atheism?
2. Why is it difficult to reject the fact that the universe has moral qualities?
3. What is the importance of human choice and subsequent consequences?

CHAPTER 9

THE PROBLEM OF BEAUTY

When we are attracted by the harmony, order and serenity of nature, so as to feel at home in it and confirmed by it, then we speak of its beauty; when, however, as on some wind-blown mountain crag, we experience the vastness, the power, the threatening majesty of the natural world, and feel our own littleness in the face of it, then we should speak of the sublime. Both these responses are elevating; both lift us out of the ordinary utilitarian thoughts that dominate our practical lives.

—ROGER SCRUTON, *BEAUTY*

Over the years, my husband and I have tried to get back to experience the beauty of the Pacific Northwest as much as possible. We've been a bit limited by time and resources. One year, however, we had an opportunity to drive Pacific Highway 101 from the Southern California coast to the

Northern Oregon coast. It was a sunny week, and we made no plans other than to drive until we got tired or until we wanted to spend time somewhere. Our schedule entailed that we had long hours on the road to think and talk about life in general. At times on the trip, I reveled in being back home. At other times, the natural beauty combined with joyful memories of my childhood overwhelmed me. What wasn't supposed to happen, though, was another gripe session. But somehow I found myself caught up in anger and grief.

"You know, Roger," I said. "It's been really hard being away from all this for so long."

"Yeah, I know."

"Do you really? Do you really understand what it's like to live away from the place you love so much? We've not moved away from your childhood home. We're basically still there. Just a little further south." Roger's desire to be empathetic suddenly felt disingenuous, and I ungraciously snapped at him. "I mean, really think about that. I've lived not only away from the beautiful land that originally drew me to God but also away from the people with whom I feel welcome."

Roger knew I was wading into dangerous waters. He'd heard this lament before. He remained cautiously silent.

"I wonder what it would have been like if we had not stayed in the South after getting married. What if we had moved here? Why did we stay in the South? Isn't a man supposed to leave his parents and cleave to his wife? Why didn't we come back to my home?"

"Jo, that's a lot. You know we couldn't afford to move."

"I don't believe you. We could've made it happen. People have done crazier things."

"Well, remember we looked for ministry positions up here.

There just wasn't much to be found in the Southern Baptist Convention of the Pacific Northwest at that time."

The mention of our denomination as a reason for, in my mind, why we were "stuck" in the southern United States was the exact wrong direction to take this conversation. Roger hit a land mine.

"You took me away from all of this. *You were the Baptist.* I was just a new Christian. I didn't know the difference between a Baptist and a Catholic. Nor did I know I would never come back to my people and my state. I didn't know how narrow-minded and ridiculous the Baptists in our churches were going to be! You knew it. You knew I didn't fit in, and yet you forced me to try to fit anyway!"

Boom! That marriage-wrecking land mine exploded with all the force of a desperate soul looking for something, or someone, to blame.

Roger was now angry. "That's entirely uncharitable."

The truth of his statement didn't go unnoticed, but I hated that he was right. I didn't speak.

"We got ourselves in a problem," Roger continued. "We had a baby at a young age. We couldn't just up and go wherever we wanted. We both had to find work and do so immediately to support our family, while finishing up college. I was raised Baptist. I didn't know anything else. That was Christianity to me. I tried to do what was best for our family."

And then came the awkward silence—the moment when I should have apologized for being ridiculous. Yet I truly felt hopeless about our situation in the church. Something was missing, and being back in the grandeur of the mountainous coastline was aggravating that something.

Full of pride and not understanding what truly bothered me,

I could only manage a short, curt response. "Sometimes I hate the church. I hate that she indiscriminately puts things down that I find beautiful and that she takes away things I love."

From the look on his face, I could tell my statement hurt Roger more intensely than the previous bomb, but I didn't know what else to say. I was so angry—so angry with our situation and the church.

"It's not just where we live. I don't fit into the church culture."

"Jo, you have friends . . . not everything has been bad . . . you've been able to do some great work . . ."

"Yes, and I appreciate that. But have I ever really shown my church friends who I am? No. Because I get pushback whenever I allow a small glimpse into my interior life. For example, remember that musical I put together using the soundtrack? Remember the comment the pastor made about my dancers?"

Of course, I knew Roger remembered. The pastor's comment was a turning point for me. I had created a dance scene representing John 1:1–5:

> In the beginning was the Word, and the Word was with God, and the Word was God. He was with God in the beginning. Through him all things were made; without him nothing was made that has been made. In him was life, and that life was the light of all mankind. The light shines in the darkness, and the darkness has not overcome it. (NIV)

In my scene, the dancers began in a folded position and slowly unraveled to reveal a candle light. It was my visual representation of the beauty of God's creative act, bringing light into the world.

The pastor came to me the night before our performance,

after dress rehearsal, and told me that the dance costumes wouldn't work. I didn't know how to respond, because I had dancers dressed in full leotard with two sets of full-length skirts over top just to be considerate of the conservative culture of the church. We'd rehearsed in front of the choir, musicians, and tech crew many times, and this was the first I'd heard of a costuming problem. When I didn't respond, he decided to elucidate the problem: "Well, the outfits won't work. They are slutty."

"Roger, he said my work was 'slutty.' Let that soak in for a moment. What I thought was a beautiful and intentional choice for an expression of worship in the church was compared to *a slut*, a woman of 'multiple casual sexual partners.' My offering was considered sexually perverse. That was violating. And the pastor didn't think a thing of it. He's just getting the problem fixed. That's what I mean when I say I don't fit in."

"What I thought was a beautiful offering in worship of God was taken as sexual perversion. Why would that thought even enter his mind? Why use *that* word? If that is the way the church views what I think is beautiful, then I'm a complete foreigner to the body of Christ. What do I possibly have in common with any of them? How could I ever trust Christians with my thoughts and feelings when they have such a completely different view and such little verbal restraint?"

Roger's anger subsided a little as he heard the story retold that day in the car. He knew the incident well, as he had to deal with my rage the evening it happened. He knew I felt betrayed and used. He saw the change in my relationship with the Christian community at this church. Compounding my frustration was confusion, because there was absolutely no teaching on beauty or artistic appreciation in the church—ever. The church didn't teach what art or beauty was for, nor how to appreciate it, but instead, leaders and members cast a "Church Lady" look of suspicion on anything artistic that wasn't familiar church hymnody or pageantry. I had more instruction on art appreciation in my fifth grade schooling! And yet this was the bride of Christ, the redeemed, the light of the world!

You might consider it somewhat childish or trite of me to let one comment affect me so greatly, and I would understand. However, it exemplifies the troublesome attitudes and behaviors I found in church life. The pastor didn't just reject my costuming on a whim. He had a lifetime of making choices based on a philosophy to which he either consciously or subconsciously adhered that led to that moment. He didn't appear to know the difference between something beautiful, gentle, and subtle with something that was overtly sexually perverse. Rather, he seemed to view the female form as an object of sexuality, and, therefore, slutty if not dressed in baggy clothing (which is how he "fixed" the problem). I had grown up watching ballerinas and dancers, without a shred of this kind of thinking. *Why did I continue in the church when it felt so unwelcome for who I am?*

I watched the waves of the ocean hit some rocks far below the highway as we drove on. There was a thick silence in the car.

"Mary Jo, I'm sorry. I'm sorry that happened to you. I don't think that way about you or about your creativity. I know there are others in the church who really enjoyed the performance. I know people were moved deeply by your vision of the creation. It was beautiful. You know that pastor was wrong." A tear rolled down my face as he said, "You know that we have a limited experience in the church. Not all churches are like what we've experienced."

I looked at him, red-eyed, and said, "I'm so sorry, Roger. It's not your fault." I wanted to say more, but I felt like I should leave it there. For years, Roger had borne the brunt of my disappointment of living in an environment that felt foreign to me. How could I aptly apologize for dumping all of that on him? I couldn't.

I didn't even know what I longed for. Where did I think I belonged? What in the crashing waves and rugged cliffs spoke so powerfully that it evoked such a visceral reaction? I seemed to be grieving as though I'd experienced an untimely death or some great loss. I was like a frustrated child screaming, "I hate you!" because he doesn't know how to express what he's feeling, and *hate* is the strongest word he can think of to put to the powerful emotions he's experiencing. Here I was—an angry child unable to put into words my emotions. I couldn't even say if there was any merit to my indignation.

We pulled into a small Northern California town to stay the night. As we settled into our room, I reflected back on the day. *Sheesh, Roger didn't "do" this to me. Something's missing, and I don't know how to explain it. He shouldn't be the fall guy for my inability to aptly formulate the problem.* As I lamented the treatment of my sweet guy, I fell asleep to the lonely ring of a coastal buoy and the crashing of waves on the rocks below.

TWO PROFESSORS

Two men have helped me think through the issue of what drew me toward God and what I found missing in the church community: John Mark Reynolds and Phil Tallon. Both gentlemen are scholars who study the topic of beauty, its purpose, its objectivity, and its use as an argument for God's existence. Both men have changed the way I interpreted my church experience and helped me discover what was missing from my experience.

I met John Mark Reynolds the summer after the "slutty" comment incident. He was the professor in my apologetics degree program who first introduced me to the role of beauty in a Christian's life. Dr. Reynolds is not like any other person I've ever met. He's a philosopher who can think and write at the deepest levels, but who will also dress up in full costume to attend an opening night of a *Star Wars* movie. He can build entire Christian schools, kindergarten through college, from the ground up, but he also cares about the subtleties of an individual's life and struggles. He has an accessible brilliance that is rare to find.

That summer, I sat in Dr. Reynolds's Cultural Apologetics class as he began his first day of lectures on Christian ethics and the value of beauty. "The central objective of this course is to present apologetics as a unifying discipline. All truth, goodness, and beauty is God's, and so an apologist is one who can show the Godward nature of all of culture, of human things. We see God and so see our humanity. We see our humanity and rejoice in human things and so worship the God who made humankind."

> **"God is the source of all truth, goodness, and beauty, and all three originate in the unity of God's very being."**
>
> Philip Tallon, *The Poetics of Evil*, 74.

Wow. This is going to be an interesting class! He speaks so differently from anyone I've ever encountered. It's like he's painting an actual picture with his words. Who talks like that?

Dr. Reynolds went on to explain that the evangelical church has moved away from teaching on beauty as objective and from a commitment to beauty as an end in itself. "In rightly rejecting hedonism, we have also mistakenly rejected joy. We thought to avoid the sin of wastefulness but have fallen into the equal sin of stinginess. Philosophy and our actions are in a biconditional relationship. We develop philosophical justifications for our actions, and our actions shape our philosophy. If we believe beauty is subjective, it allows, and suggests, that we either can privilege our garish taste or 'save money' on beauty because it is frill. In many places, utility rules over all."

Now we're starting to get somewhere! I was originally drawn to God, in large part, by a sense of wonder at all the beauty in the world. When I became an evangelical, I found a lack of attention to beauty, as Reynolds suggested. Perhaps that is one reason I've been so disappointed in many evangelical church buildings that value function, or utility, *entirely* over form. My fellow Baptists have often called their churches "Baptist barns" because their structures lack beauty. Now, I do understand that sometimes a strip mall, an old Wal-Mart, or the only building available to you is where you church plant. I'm thinking more of those who do so little to beautify the building *because of stinginess* (not considering beauty worthwhile), not just due to location, cultural appropriateness, and cost.

Reynolds had moved on: "Beauty is so great, like truth, that a quest for beauty, just like the quest for truth, can do great harm to a soul that goes the wrong way. Yet, just as we cannot give up truth, so we cannot give up on beauty. There is danger in pursuing the beautiful exactly because there is power. However, conversely, the result of a loss of beauty has been a utilitarian view of not only buildings and art, but also bodies [people]."

As he said these words, powerful emotions stirred in me. *He's hitting on the problem I had at church. Women viewed in a utilitarian way as bodies . . . whose function is to produce sexual arousal in others.*

When Reynolds gave the class a break, I shot out of my seat to speak with him. I shared with him my recent experience in church and how the pastor had used the word *slutty* to describe my work. I explained how debased I felt by his wording.

Dr. Reynolds gave a heavyhearted sigh. "Mary Jo, the pastor has deeply erred. Although I wasn't there and don't know him, he may have erred because to him, physical beauty was for one thing (sexuality). Beauty causes love to arise, but love is not about owning or possessing. It seems to me that his language choice, bad enough as it was, pointed to a denigration of the body and a failure to understand beauty."

Funny how such a few words spoken in truth and love could so suddenly rock my world. Dr. Reynolds put words to the anger I felt at the view of the dancers and of my offering. He had summed up the misunderstanding and confusion in just a few sentences.

I felt tears welling up, but I had just met Dr. Reynolds, and I didn't want to make our meeting weird. I stood there in silence, looking at him, trying to process the depth of what he had just said to me. At my nonresponse, Reynolds asked, "Would you mind sharing your story with our class? I think your perspective in this situation would be valuable for us to hear."

With his invitation, I snapped back into the conversation. "Sure, I'd love to."

Of course, I wasn't being entirely honest. Though I didn't mind speaking in front of the group, this wound was obviously still bleeding. Confusion and hurt had been my companions for a while on this matter. I was afraid of being mean-spirited or of tearing up. I didn't really know many of my classmates yet, and I didn't want their first impression of me to be a teary-eyed, emotional thirty-year-old woman.

However, when our class reconvened, I was able to give a succinct retelling of the incident without adding much commentary, and then take my seat. Dr. Reynolds bounced off of my story to continue his teaching. He used the pastor's interpretation of women's physical beauty as "good for one thing" to focus on women as having been objectified for profit and the subsequent distortion of beauty in our society. He discussed how he began to see the problems in his own thinking about beauty.

"I realized that some problems in my own life were caused by objectification and thinking that beauty was 'for me.' That needed to change. I also looked for the roots of this, not as an excuse, but to keep weeding it out. I realized that, by accident, free markets allowed an irresponsible use of images to sell product. Soon, *images* of people outnumbered, for the first time in human history, *seeing* people. Sadly, making beauty an object and using it to sell has resulted in great harm. As an example, 'a look' came to dominate and so one 'look' was beautiful and all others were not. This was particularly hard on women of color or anyone who did not fit 'the it girl' of the moment. People have been told they do not have beauty simply because they could not move products in an ad. We have done this much less with men. However, when the error is exposed, we can bring about healing."

I wondered if this was actually the root of the problem I encountered with the pastor of my church. I wondered how many pastors, Christian men, or Christians in general, had this view—even unknowingly. If beauty is reduced to some utilitarian purpose, even without intentionally doing so, it would seem to produce the experiences I've had. I was getting the vibe from the church that a woman's beauty was for a man's enjoyment, which is why her beauty must be carefully controlled. It's a distraction and temptation.

Contrast this with a view that a woman's beauty reflects the orderly thought of God, who created and designed the universe with all its beauty. Why not, then, see a woman's beauty as pointing to the existence of God? Why not see beauty, in general, as a marker of design or order, something that is supposed to be enjoyed, yes, but enjoyed for the purpose of reflection on the

Creator himself, the artist? Why reduce beauty to sexual utility and hedonistic pleasure?

Reynolds gave me a starting point for my thinking. However, I was distracted by my growing apologetics ministry with David and Nabeel, as well as writing an apologetics study and book. Soon I was speaking nearly every other week, either on the radio, at a church, or at an apologetics event. Further, Dr. Reynolds became provost at a Christian university in Houston, and he asked me to come on board to develop an apologetics degree. So at that point in my life I didn't take the time to dig into the importance of beauty in drawing us to God, nor did I explore why the lack of an understanding of beauty in the church caused me so much angst. Years later, however, I met and spoke with another professor who helped me to put words to my frustrations.

I met Dr. Phil Tallon when he was hired as the chair over the department of apologetics at the university where, just a few years earlier, Dr. Reynolds himself had hired me as a professor. Phil is a professor of theology who is as hip as he is smart. He teaches the film and apologetics class and is the kind of guy who can seamlessly move between discussing his family, C. S. Lewis, great works of art, horror films, and Christian doctrine. Tallon writes extensively on the issue of beauty, so I hoped he could help me figure some things out.

I caught up with Phil at his office, only two doors down from mine in the School of Christian Thought. He frequently leaves his door open so friendly faces can pop in for a visit, so I decided to drop in. His desk was full of paperwork, as usual, and I could see from his computer screen that he had multiple projects going. As soon as he saw me, however, he moved back from his desk, smiled, and gave his usual cheery greeting, "Hey, MJ, what's up?"

Though Phil had been a friend for a few years, as the head of my department he was still one of my bosses. I wasn't sure how to approach this issue. *As my supervisor, he had to evaluate my teaching skills and knowledge every year, so it felt a little nerve-wracking to admit I didn't know this thing that I felt like I should know by now.* Still, I was banking on the fact that Phil was a great guy, someone I'd be friends with even if we didn't work together.

"Hey, Phil, I've been thinking on what originally drew me to God, and I'm having some problems finding the words. Do you have some time to work through this with me?"

"Actually, yes. You caught me at a pretty good time."

"Great!" I settled into a chair and began. "I wanted to talk with you because I know of your background in the argument from beauty. I thought you might help me understand and express how it was that beauty was one of the factors that drew me toward God. I was impressed by both the natural beauty of my childhood home and the beauty of the arts in which I participated at school, like band and choir. My mom and dad were both lovers of the outdoors, science buffs, and huge arts enthusiasts. They took our family camping all over the Northwest and to as many musical programs, plays, and museums as they could. Plus, my dad enjoyed sharing his knowledge on the latest scientific discoveries. They definitely passed on a love of all these things to me, and I feel as though God somehow used these things to draw me to himself. But that's pretty much what I've got to offer. Can you help me?"

"Yeah, MJ, I think I can help. The wildness of the woods, the beauty of the mountains, the sublime nature of sunsets—all these things are the visible presence of God in the world through his creation. God made creation to reflect parts of who he is." Phil referred to Romans 1:20: "For since the creation of the world God's invisible qualities—his eternal power and divine nature—have been clearly seen" (NIV). Then he explained that the beautiful complexity of an ecosystem gives us a glimpse of the complexity of the three-in-one God. The sublimity and grandeur of the mountains reflect God's magnificence and power. Sunsets reflect the radiance of the divine light.

"You're seeing aspects of God's beauty in these created things. You're enjoying the thing itself, but your love of it was awakening a desire for more of it. Artistry is good, but if you want more you have to go toward the source." Phil then offered an example he knew would resonate with me and my love of the *Star Wars* saga. "For instance, I actually enjoy *Star Wars* movies more when I realize that it's a lesser good pointing me onto the greater good found in God. The movies can only give me a certain amount of satisfaction and pleasure, because it is not the originating source of satisfaction and pleasure."

He explained that as fallen creatures, we tend to settle for the goodness of created things rather than pushing ourselves to search for the source of goodness. (Or as Romans 1:23 puts it, we "worshiped and served created things rather than the Creator" [NIV].) What we really need to look for, he said, are the ultimate things, the source of the good, the love that fulfills our deepest longings. He concluded, "It sounds like you were searching for the ultimate thing, the source of what you loved."

I nodded enthusiastically. "Wow, Phil, I would *never* have put it like that." *He pieced that together from what I said?* All I had been able to do was question the purpose of all this beauty in the world. His thoughts reminded me of what John Mark Reynolds said, that the love of beauty awakens a desire for more of it, the desire to find that which is truly loved . . . the source of beauty.

Phil smiled at my response, paused a moment, and waited to see where I was going next. When he realized I wasn't ready to move on just yet, he expanded a little more on the same idea.

"The things you experienced in the arts and in the natural realm bear the artist's mark, a mark that draws us upward to the source . . . to the artist himself. It's a common occurrence in our human experience that when we love the work of an artist, such as a musician, an actor, or a film director, we begin to find out everything we can about that artist. We are drawn to them, which is the artistry drawing us toward the artist."

"I think I get what you are saying, but, Phil, I've never heard any teaching like this in my entire life. You see, when I became a part of the church, I felt like I experienced a bait and switch. God drew me with his mark of beauty in the world, but after joining an evangelical church I never heard any mention of beauty. What happened?"

"Well, there's a lot of background to the story of 'what happened' that goes back to the Reformation and the iconoclast movements, but also to how those movements developed in the American frontier. Without getting into a lengthy history lesson, I think we can look at this issue in the current evangelical church in America."

Phil explained that the Bible teaches that God is good, true, and beautiful. Then he pointed to something about these objective realities of God that I've never considered. Evangelicals are not currently relativistic about truth and we are not relativistic about morals. We believe in truth and falsity and also in right and wrong. Yet when it comes to the third aspect of God, his beauty, we've taken a *secular view* that beauty is **relativistic**, or solely in the eye of the beholder. We've adopted this view as if there is no problem in doing so.

Relativism: The belief that knowledge, truth, and morality exist in relation to culture, society, or historical context, and are not absolute.

Adapted from Lexico, s.v. "relativism," www.lexico.com/en/definition/relativism.

However, there *is* a problem with doing so: because the Bible talks about God's goodness, truth, *and beauty* as **objective realities**. If we really believe God is beautiful and we believe God is real, we should take beauty seriously. If we don't properly appreciate the beautiful, we can't properly appreciate God. Thus, we need to be wary of using a secular mentality to view this objective reality of God's beauty.

My experiences in the church, specifically related to the problem of beauty, were beginning to make more sense. Phil has a great way of making hard-to-grasp concepts quite accessible. I asked, "So if we are missing this attribute of God, what are we missing out on? Is it just that we don't understand the nature of God?"

Objective realities: Things that exist independently of us; the existence of these things are not dependent on the subjective perceptions of humans.

"Well, let's look at it this way: the first question of the Westminster Confession[1] is, what is the chief aim of man? Man's chief end is to glorify God and to enjoy him forever. Enjoyment is an aesthetic mode of appreciation. We've focused almost entirely on Christian believing and Christian living, but not on Christian loving . . . and loving rightly. We've neglected the training of our loves and the formation of Christian taste. Part of Christianity is appreciating things appropriately.

"If we appreciate things rightly, the arts can really help us to shape our emotions and affections. Good artistry helps to form us into the people God wants us to be so that we can enjoy him and his creation rightly. But we've adopted a view that there is no right response. So I think that's one of the important aspects of

---

1   From the Shorter Catechism.

Christianity, and of the worship of God, that you found missing. The very objective reality that drew you so strongly to God is the one that is most often neglected in our teaching and formation in the evangelical church."

"Perhaps I felt its absence without understanding that was the issue?"

"Yes, that could be."

"But, Phil, how would I ever discuss the impact of the lack of teaching on this objective reality without sounding like a snob?"

I was dead serious about this question. I was worried I'd come across as an esoteric academic if I began to teach on the lack of beauty in the church.

"I think you have to learn to recognize what's missing, why it isn't there, and then find the beauty that is there as well. It's not just about pointing out what we're missing, but also learning to see what is there. The evangelical church is not bereft of beauty. I could point to the church tradition of hymnody as an example of beauty.

"However, there is a trend in the evangelical church to reduce the value of artistic endeavors exclusively to how they serve the true and the good. We tend to view the music, for instance, as an amplification of the sermon rather than as a testimony to the objective beauty of God himself. This view is why people believe that the lyrics of a song are what determine whether it's Christian or not, which is a reductionist view of beauty, reducing beauty to the utility it serves. Rather, all beauty evidences the beauty of God himself, not just things that use words, and that's a point we've been missing."

Learn to recognize what's missing, but then also find the beauty that is there. I had been busy trying to figure out why I didn't fit into the evangelical church, and weathering the resultant hurt.

I had been particularly grieved when church members simplistically rejected my work or made demeaning comments about it. All I saw was hypocrisy from those who professed to follow the Beautiful One. Talking with Phil helped me to see that if a person hasn't been trained in those artistic mediums, nor taught to appreciate them, it's unrealistic to expect them to enjoy them. He even mentioned that he could understand the suspicion of those who encountered an art form with which they had limited experience. He still believed the church could use some theological work in this area (some backtracking, perhaps), but he could see why people had such strong emotional responses. *Yet to me that just complicated things! It was easier to box up my fellow evangelicals into a category and then say that they just didn't understand me.* What I had seen as a black-and-white issue was now becoming a complicated one involving various church cultures and traditions, as well as differing individual education and backgrounds.

Phil also gave me the language I couldn't find on my own about what drew me to God in the first place. In part, I was attracted by my wonder at the world's beauty, which is reflective of God's beauty. Consequently, when I became involved in a church life in which beauty had been reduced to utility and subjectivity, I felt remorse and grief. Yet I didn't know how to frame my sense of loss or how to determine if the loss was even real. I decided to chalk it up to cultural differences. However, if the church was neglecting a part of *God's nature*, then I wasn't just experiencing a cultural difference. There's a real discipleship failing here that has left evangelicals with a missing piece of their theology and spiritual life.

So many things were beginning to make sense from just this introduction to the argument from beauty. One thing was for sure: beauty wasn't going to offer me a quick exit from the church. Rather, she invited me to look for an objectively beautiful God. In a chapter Phil wrote arguing for the existence of God, he utilized objective beauty as the basis of his argument:

> If the Christian God exists, who is beautiful in His very nature, we would expect there to be objective beauty. Because this God is the creator of the world, and it reflects His nature, we would expect the world to be invested with a great amount of objective beauty. We would also expect, given the claims of Christian theology, that beauty would be integrated with other values in a way that reflects the ultimate union of Beauty with Truth and Goodness in the nature of God. Further, because of both our fallenness and the ongoing grace of God to give access to basic perception of value, we would expect perception of beauty to be difficult-yet-achievable. It would be difficult to judge rightly in a fully consistent manner, especially as regards more complex aesthetic objects, yet we should retain a capacity to discern beauty, one that deepens as we grow in our knowledge of God and his revelation in Christ. There *is* a great amount of objective beauty (and it is integrated-and-knowable-yet-difficult), therefore beauty is evidence, not just for theism, but for Christian theism.[2]

There's a lot to think about in just that one quote. There is a great amount of beauty in the world, and not only is it evidence for God, but it is also something that continues to push

---

2   Phil Tallon, "The Theistic Argument from Beauty and Play," in *Two Dozen or So Arguments for God,* eds. Jerry L. Walls and Trent Doughtery (New York: Oxford University Press, 2018), 334–35.

me onward and upward toward the source. Beauty is that which draws me toward God and, at times, the lack of beauty in the church is what pushes me away. It is such a tumultuous relationship, and it is a risk to commit to a beautiful God, especially with his not-always-so-beautiful bride. There are a lot of human failings along the way. Even today, I still feel a sting when God's beauty is ignored or perverted. Despite all that, am I willing to take the risk?

• CONSIDERATIONS •

1. Reflect on your own experience in the church. How have you been taught to encounter or engage with beauty?
2. What is one practical way the church can teach about the beauty of God?
3. How can beauty help us understand the nature of God?
4. What is the purpose of beauty in the church?

CHAPTER 10

INSTRUCTIONS ON HOW TO BE HUMAN

Even if not overtly admitted, the search for truth is
nevertheless hauntingly present, propelled by the
need for incontrovertible *answers* to four inescapable
questions, those dealing with origin, meaning, morality,
and destiny. No thinking person can avoid this search,
and it can only end when one is convinced that the
answers espoused are true.

—RAVI ZACHARIAS, *CAN MAN LIVE WITHOUT GOD*

"Let's try a run on your own now. You've got the basics down."

The ski instructor smiled at Roger and me through a blizzard-like blur of snow. He'd just finished teaching us an introductory ski lesson, a surprise gift from Roger to celebrate our wedding anniversary. Now it was time for us to try out our newly acquired skills. I had skied a couple times before as a teenager. My older brother was quite skilled at skiing and had taught me the basics. Roger, on the other hand, was a complete novice.

As we all stood at the top of a fairly flat ski run, Roger began to laugh. "Well, I still haven't figured out how to do the turns."

"So, what are you going to do, Mr. Sharp?" I cocked my head and gave him a coy smile.

"Well, since I can't turn, I'm going to head straight down the run. I'll see you at the bottom or however far I make it."

Roger paralleled his skis, pointed them directly at the run, crouched down a little, and shoved off with his ski polls. I yelled out to him some unhelpful but good-hearted encouragement, "You can do it. Try the pizza formation to turn! Lean! Remember to lean!"

As we watched, Roger picked up quite a bit of speed. But he didn't turn. Within just a minute, Roger began to lose control. He wobbled. He bobbled. One of his poles fell. Down he went with a pole here and a ski there and a glove way over there. I let out a loud "Ohhhhhhhh!"

For the moment, there was a pause as the ski instructor and I took in the spectacularly comical fall we had just witnessed. Then the instructor looked at me with a raised eyebrow and said dryly, "Now that's what we call a yard sale . . . 'cause it's all laid out."

Roger just couldn't turn. Though the instructions he received should have worked in theory, the reality is that he couldn't turn. The lived-out version of the instructions he received was much different than the outcome. So what was the problem? Was there something wrong in the instructions, or did something go wrong on the receiving end? Or was there another problem? The hard part of this dilemma is figuring out what went wrong, where it went wrong, and why it went wrong. Roger doesn't *want* to ski poorly; rather, he wants to do well. Roger knows what to do, he's been given the education and opportunity to do what is right, but he keeps failing to turn, and thus he keeps wiping out.

To me, Roger's ski dilemma reflects an even greater dilemma of humankind. The more I learn about and experience humans and their history—myself included—the more I realize that no matter how many "ski lessons" or opportunities and education you give an individual, he or she often still crashes and burns.

Being human is an odd experience. I go about my daily living as if there were some kind of instructions to follow, and yet I desire to do everything my own way. When I fail to live up to the instructions given—as I inevitably will—I'm left wondering what went wrong. Sometimes I don't even notice that something went wrong until I've hurt another person. *Why can't I just do what is right? Why do I continue to be my own worst enemy, my greatest hindrance, in situations where I know what to do? Why do I seem to twist the teaching I receive and end up doing something unintentionally hurtful, harmful, or hateful?* Humans seem to have some instructions, but don't seem to follow them. Worse still, we sometimes rationalize that the instructions are faulty and try to make our own sense of things.

As I considered my miserable state in the church, I had to deeply reflect on a life without Christianity. I had to consider the answers to my questions outside of any Christian teachings. To leave Christianity would be to embrace an alternative view of what it meant to be human. I would have to agree with a perspective that said that Christianity's instructions for how to be human were all wrong.[1] Christianity claims that the instructions given to

---

1   I'm using "instructions" here in relation to my ski-instructions metaphor. However, I do not intend to give the impression with this metaphor that humans come into the world as a *tabula rasa*, or as a completely blank slate, so that the Bible tells us what we should do from the point of that blank slate. Rather, the Bible not only instructs us

humankind are true, but there's something generally wrong on the receiving end. Conversely, a view that leaves out God claims there's generally nothing wrong on the receiving end, but rather the instructions given by Christians are faulty.

To get to truth, one must dump erroneous teachings, freeing up the mind to see truth. But what exactly does *that handbook* look like? Further, in considering the atheist view, what are the atheist instructions for how to be human, and how do we know these instructions are true? What has been my experience with these teachings? Without going into great detail, I'll try to outline those views here.

HUMANS: A HIGHER ORDER OF ANIMAL

Personhood entails a personal being, "a conscious agent with the capacity to think, feel, choose, and act—in contrast to an unconscious principle or substance that operates by blind, automatic forces (such as the forces of nature)."

Nancy Pearcey,
Finding Truth, 29.

Some popular atheists seem to guide us toward understanding ourselves as a higher order of animal, with advanced cognitive abilities and not much more. Consequently, we shouldn't think more highly of the human race than of any other species on earth. Peter Singer writes in his famous work *Unsanctifying Human Life*, "The doctrine of the sanctity of human life, as it is normally understood, has at its core a discrimination of species and nothing else."[2] He argues that humans

---

as to what we should do as humans but also as to *what we are* as humans. The two types of instruction are inextricably tied to one another.

2 Peter Singer, *Unsanctifying Human Life* (Oxford: Blackwell, 2002), 221.

should be able to provide mercy killings for those who have little to no chance for a meaningful life, similar to the mercy killing of a beloved family dog or horse. To make this argument, Singer separates biological humanness, a material trait, from **personhood**, which is a metaphysical trait. Personhood, to Singer, is constituted by the *acquisition* of certain cognitive abilities: at the least, consciousness, the ability to relate to one's surroundings, rationality, and self-awareness. Human value and worth are then based on the current status of these abilities, without which a human would cease to be a person.

Take Singer's view all the way to its logical end, and a human is only as valuable as her capability to exercise these abilities. As we can empirically verify, some humans hold certain cognitive abilities, like math skills or musical skills, at a higher level than other humans. Thus, if I were to qualify a person as having the right to life by their abilities, then, consequently, some humans would qualify as more valuable than others due to their more advanced cognitive abilities. The result is an implicit caste system that would devastate the human community.

Another problem is that when a person lacks these cognitive abilities—for example, when they lack consciousness—then that human has lost their personhood and therefore the protections offered to human persons (such as the right to life). Yet such a view leads to disastrous consequences, as humans lose consciousness when they fall asleep or fall into a coma. Every night billions of humans would lose their right to life based on normal human sleep patterns. It sounds absurd or like a slippery slope, but I have taken Singer's view all the way to its logical end. I haven't afforded Singer any "Get-out-of-jail-free cards" for his views.

Do I agree with Singer's views on what it means to be human? By now, you know that I obviously do not. A more appropriate question for me would be did I *ever* agree with Singer's views? I never have. I wouldn't have agreed with this philosophy even before grounding human value in the doctrine of the image of God. For even in young adulthood, I believed that human beings had some significant value that stands above the animal kingdom. I held that human beings were valuable *for the kind of thing that they are, just as they are.* As a person who lacked belief in God, I didn't have a thought-out grounding for my view. I just believed this was the right way of understanding and valuing people.

Singer challenges humans to dispense with religious (specifically Christian) notions of the "sanctity of human life" and replace them with a utilitarian view of human beings. Any human who is not able to demonstrate Singer's outlined basics of cognitive abilities are of less value. He writes, "But if an infant cannot value, or want, its own continued existence, then the loss of life for a newborn infant must be less significant than the loss of life for an older child or adult who wants to go on living. This conclusion has, as we shall see, far reaching consequences for our treatment of seriously ill or handicapped infants."[3] Singer has already worked out the implications of his own philosophy, creating a caste system of humans based on levels of cognitive abilities.

What then are Singer's instructions of how to be human if there were certain things wrong with me? I should be "mercifully" put down. Killed. Singer's utilitarian view of what it means to be human ends in death for those he deems unworthy of life. If there is nothing special about humanity and no good or evil in the universe, then there are quick fixes to help the human race become unfettered by the less-fit few, producing more pleasure

---

3 Singer, *Unsanctifying Human Life*, 240.

for the most number of people. The end game seems to be maximizing pleasure for certain privileged people.

If I were to try to live this view out in real life, I would have to get rid of my unfortunately ski-dysfunctional husband, who cannot maximize my skiing pleasure to bring me a greater amount of good. Rather, because Roger's skiing abilities have little to no chance of providing a meaningful skiing life, I am justified in dumping him and moving on to maximize my pleasure.[4]

HUMANS: JUST A COLLECTION OF ATOMS

Another contemporary understanding of humans is the materialistic view espoused by Richard Dawkins. Dawkins believes that only physical things have existence. There is no immaterial or "spiritual" realm, so humans are reducible to their material makeup. As I pointed out in chapter 8, Dawkins believes we do nothing but dance to the music of our DNA. Materialism poses several problems in what it means to be human.

First, if I'm just a collection of atoms, organized a certain way to do

Materialism is "the belief that everything is made of matter and energy, with no 'immaterial' entities like souls, spirits, or supernatural gods. In addition, materialists do not believe in 'metaphysical transcendence,' or any layer of being that goes beyond the material world."

Pearcey, Finding Truth, 29.

---

4   Of course, this is an exaggeration or hyperbole of Singer's argument for the sake of some fun amid discussing a philosophical view that entails quite morbid implications. I assume Singer would adamantly disagree with my analogy, saying that I should simply stop trying to make Roger ski in order to honor Roger's preferences and happiness.

certain things, then I cannot actually have free will or autonomy: not in emotion, desire, thought, choice, or action. At the end of the day, Dawkins is declaring that everything is determined by our genetic predispositions. In doing so, he undermines the very thing I think he's trying to protect with his aggressive campaign against religion. Dawkins lectures us on why we should choose to elevate science over faith while holding a position that says we cannot really choose anything at all!

Second, Dawkins's view gives him no basis for complaining about religion in the first place. Dawkins seems to be truly upset at the horrors of the world, as am I. For me, the world moved very far away from God's original good creation of it. My horror is based on what God made versus what we did with the creation. Yet on what basis is Dawkins horrified? According to a materialist view, what we see in the world is just the way things are as the universe marches on in an ever-evolving process. Here again, he pulls the rug out from under himself. If humans are thinking and acting out what is genetically predetermined, then even Dawkins's reasoning, actions, and moral judgments are the result of dancing to his own DNA, and therefore not the result of a life of reflection and reasoning well.[5]

Third, what does his view offer as a means of hope in the face of the horrors of the world? Not much. Hope, in this philosophical stew, is an illusion. The magic atheist fairy sprinkles words like *hope, good, justice,* and *value* into our language. She's quite convenient, because she garnishes our vernacular with

---

5 Note, I am specifically addressing materialistic determinism. I am not here engaging in the Christian scholarly debate on God's foreknowledge and humankind's freedom. Although some Christian viewpoints come closer to determinism, I am currently unaware of any that fully align with materialistic determinism. I'm also not addressing nonreductionist materialism at this time.

these words and then cheerfully tells us to start enjoying our lives without God as her tiny fairy wings carry her away into unknown realms.[6] However, she always forgets to do the serious heavy lifting required for giving those words meaning and consequence.

Even agnostics such as nineteenth-century philosopher Arthur Schopenhauer and twenty-first-century scholar Bart Ehrman determine that because of evil in the world, and the hopelessness that results, the answer is that we humans should just make more of an effort to be good to one another. I get the sense that I'm supposed to just do good on the basis that it's considered good by a Western academic like Dawkins or the other New Atheists.[7] There is little to no consideration for what "the good life" is or how I'm supposed to recognize it, even though the topic has been discussed by philosophers for over two thousand years.

For all the positive thinking coming from these skeptics, I cannot get around this conclusion: there is no reason to "buck up, little camper" if there is nothing other than the materialistic universe. Rather, we are faced with oppression, pain, suffering, evil, destruction, and death . . . and it carries on like this until the universe itself dies a spectacularly lonely death. As King Solomon once said in recognizing the existential angst of such a world, "I thought the dead who are already dead more fortunate than the living who are still alive. But better than both is he who has not yet been and has not seen the evil deeds that are done under the sun" (Ecclesiastes 4:2–3). Faced with a life full of suffering and without meaning, Solomon concludes it's better to have never existed.

Famous atheist philosopher Bertrand Russell didn't attempt

---

6   Really, she flies away into nonexistent realms, since she does not exist in a materialistic universe, and neither do her fanciful concepts.

7   Christopher Hitchens, Daniel Dennett, and Sam Harris.

to dress up the truth of a materialistic universe with flowery optimism:

> That man is the product of causes which had no prevision of the end they were achieving; that his origin, his growth, his hopes and fears, his loves and beliefs, are but the outcome of accidental collocations of atoms; that no fire, no heroism, no intensity of thought and feeling can preserve an individual life beyond the grave; that all labors of the ages, all the devotion, all the inspiration, all the noonday brightness of human genius are destined to extinction in the vast death of the solar system, and that the whole temple of man's achievement must inevitably be buried beneath the debris of a universe in ruins. . . . Only within the scaffolding of these truths, only on the firm foundation of unyielding despair, can the soul's habitation henceforth be safely built.[8]

There is no wishful thinking here—no atheistic fairies—but rather stark realism based in a logical conclusion deduced from his philosophical view.

So often, I encounter the tired old mantra that Christians have to make up a deity and afterlife because they cannot bear the truth of nonexistence after death. Yet simultaneously I hear atheists of my own day campaigning with slogans like "There's probably no God; now stop worrying and enjoy your life."[9] I wouldn't be so concerned with the matter if these same atheists

8 Bertrand Russell, *Why I Am Not a Christian* (New York: Simon & Schuster, 1957), 107.

9 Mark Sweeney, "ASA Clears Atheist Bus Campaign Ads," *Guardian*, January 21, 2009, www.theguardian.com/media/2009/jan/21/asa-clears-atheist-bus-ad-campaign.

didn't so often declare that they are the educated ones committed to following the truth wherever it leads. I must wonder: *Are these morbid concepts of the logical end of their thinking too burdensome to bear? How do they not see the contradictory nature of their own positive campaigning? Am I actually willing to accept such a false positive outlook and then think of myself as the "smarter" or "brighter" one? Is a positivist atheism on the way to becoming the opiate of the masses?*

Due to the inconsistencies I keep finding in contemporary atheists, I've actually grown to appreciate certain thoughts of the agnostic/atheist philosophers of the nineteenth century. For example, Arthur Schopenhauer writes about our existence as humans:

> As a reliable compass for orienting yourself in life nothing is more useful than to accustom yourself to regarding this world as a place of atonement, a sort of penal colony. When you have done this you will order your expectations of life according to the nature of things and no longer regard the calamities, sufferings, torments and miseries of life as something irregular and not to be expected but will find them entirely in order, well knowing that each of us is here being punished for his existence and each in his own particular way.[10]

He further says of the vanity of our existence:

> The most perfect manifestation of the will to live represented by the human organism, with its incomparably ingenious and

---

10 Arthur Schopenhauer, *Essays and Aphorisms* (New York: Penguin Group, 2004 [1970]), 49.

complicated machinery, must crumble to dust and its whole essence with all its striving be palpably given over at last to annihilation—this is nature's unambiguous declaration *that all the striving of this will is essentially vain*. If it were something possessing value in itself, something which ought uncondition-ally to exist, it would not have non-being as its goal.[11]

Whatever you think of Russell or Schopenhauer, at least both demonstrate some consistency in their view!

Dawkins's materialistic instructions for life are this: hate religion vehemently, have a false hope for life, and try to be the best person you can be . . . for no reason other than that Dawkins says so. You will have no reason to believe his beliefs, and even your belief is not really belief but a predetermined outcome. Your defects are hardwired, life is bleak, and annihilation is the end game. No matter what, you are the way that you are because of nature. Anything you do, or do not do, is the result of predeter-mined causal forces. Like a materialistic marionette, you move through your limited lifespan, and then either natural selection or gravity and decay will snuff you out.

But doesn't my experience of being human entail much more than Dawkins's reduction of me to simply matter? I know I'm more than a blob of atoms. I know that I matter more than matter. I see how my immaterial attitudes and thoughts affect my surroundings all the time.

HUMANS AS MEANING MAKERS

In my search for more satisfying answers from atheism, I found Michael Ruse, a contemporary atheist philosopher who seems to

---

11 Schopenhauer, *Essays and Aphorisms*, 54.

be more reasonable and thoughtful. His treatment of Christianity is more informed than the usual fare of flippant caricatures that are passed off as thoughtful and investigated. Ruse is much more open to the fact that human desires and biases get in the way of discovering truth. His atheism, as presented in *Atheism: What Everyone Needs to Know,* is no knight in shining armor battling the dreaded religion dragon for the freedom of the masses. He's willing to consider that atheism and theism aren't as polarized as contemporaries make them out to be, specifically because both involve human reasoning.

However, by the end of his work, he ends up thinking that moving on from Christianity is akin to moving on from childhood, as if all reasonable and educated adults would do the same. (I admit I have a difficult time with this common paradigm of adult Christians, since my childhood paradigm was atheist. The act of moving on as a reasonable and educated adult would, in my case, mean moving from childhood atheism to a robust Christianity.) In struggling with why so many people believe in God—even some brilliant people—his answer seems to be wrapped up in a Freudian sense of the need for a god to make sense of our world. He says of his father, "In the tense years after the Second World War, my father rather needed such a God to make sense of the awful state of the world."[12]

Here again, God is represented as a human wish-fulfillment device. He is not represented as the God whom philosophers and theologians argued over the years as the best answer to

1. why we find meaning and purpose to human life;

---

12 Michael Ruse, *Atheism: What Everyone Needs to Know* (Oxford: Oxford University Press, 2015), 62, Kindle.

2. why there is something rather than nothing;
3. what is at the origin of a universe like ours;
4. why we can trust our reasoning skills as truth-making devices;
5. why we have real hope rather than human-manufactured whims;
6. how we know what it means to be a flourishing human.

Does this all sound too biased toward Christianity? Perhaps. But the problem I had when I truly considered atheism was the inconsistency and lack of grounding for basic things like rationality, love, and hope. The atheist "book of ski instructions" is a massive book full of rationalizations about why humans don't need ski instructions; they just need to try their best to be good at skiing. The concluding instruction before you hit the slopes is a blank page. A smiling ski instructor tells you just to go for it on the slopes, because there's probably no real way to ski after all. Just get on with skiing and enjoy your life.

Here's the thing: I could do what they prescribe. I could try to give up on belief in God, pointing to all the instances of evil in the world, specifically citing the evil I've experienced in the church. I could justify walking away, because even if there is a God, his people are a bunch of jerks. Wouldn't I rather "just enjoy my life" than deal with all the messiness of humans living in community with one another? Isn't it going to be so much better on the outside of religion? The New Atheists make these bright and shiny promises. And I've lost count of how many times online atheist interactions have alluded to the same thing.

Yet the fly in the ointment remains. If I try to ski any which way I deem, and if my "way" doesn't match reality, I'm going to run into life-altering problems, as did my sweet husband on the slopes so many years ago. Dallas Willard once said, "We can think of reality as what you run into when you are wrong."[13] Roger's run into reality was a comical slip and basically not much harm done. However, on the other of the spectrum, we have a family friend who ran into a tree while downhill skiing. She ended up in a coma and when she finally awoke, she could not speak. Her run into reality was life-altering. If I try to live my life any way I think is right, I'm bound to hit something wrong and hit it hard—because of reality. If there are instructions on how to be human or what it means to be human, no amount of rationalization is going to change the outcome of failing to follow the instructions. And it seems that even when I do follow the instructions, there is still going to be trouble because of the evil in the world.

HUMANS: MADE IN THE IMAGE OF GOD

So where does that leave me? It leaves me at a point of considering whether God's instruction manual is wrong. These instructions don't deny the material aspect of humans but also don't deny, nor leave ungrounded, the immaterial aspect of humans, such as rationality, morality, love, and hope. Humans are made in the image of God. In part, this image means that we reflect some of the traits of the creative intelligence that made everything. Just like I can see attributes of the artist in his painting, so too can I see attributes of God in his creation. If God exists, this concept doesn't seem too far a stretch; rather, it would seem to

---

13 Dallas Willard, "Truth: Can We Do without It?," *Dallas Willard*, www.dwillard .org/articles/individual/truth-can-we-do-without-it.

logically flow from God's existence as creator. I observe an analogous pattern in everyday life with humans as creators of things, not exactly the same as God's creative abilities, but as reflections based on the real existence of these qualities found in God's own nature. For example, I see in human children the reflection of human parents' material and immaterial traits. Rather than the origin of such personhood traits coming out of thin air or being an accident of nature, which happens in a materialistic view,[14] the traits are grounded in a real being, giving them real existence.

God's instructions for how to be human entail a myriad of considerations, so I'm just going to share a few. Before I do, I need to share a thought on the silliness of some people's objections to God's instructions. Some people will read the Bible to mine it for commands that God has given to specific people in history and then use those commands for us today. I once read a comment that said something like, "See how far you can get through the Bible enacting God's commands before you get thrown into jail." Such a challenge is rather silly, since I do not live in a tribal setting, nor in an ancient city, as did the people of the early communities of the Bible, who fought off vicious attacks by others in order to simply live. I cannot use the specifics of the commands for that era and those societies as even close to appropriate for my own era and society. If I study the anthropology of those peoples, I might understand the overarching narrative or moral lesson from the situation, but I really would have no idea what would be proper action in those situations, as I have never lived in such an environment or faced those challenges.

Further, some authors have taken the Levitical and

---

14 The traits have no grounding as we move back in time to the origin of human beings.

Deuteronomic laws and extracted them from a serious study of their cultural-historical context or from any consideration of purpose or intention and then attempted to "live biblically" in accordance with these laws. Typically, there is no consideration for God's original relationship with man, nor for why all these laws came about, nor what it means for Jesus to say that he is the fulfillment of the law. I've seen statements such as, "If you really believe in God, why are you wearing mixed fabrics, since the Old Testament forbids it?" As ridiculous and ignorant as these statements are, they frame a cultural mindset that is as powerful as it is unthoughtful. While I tend to sympathize with the person who is angry with ignorant Christians, this is not a time to fight fire with fire. Ignorance only spawns more ignorance, not true knowledge. If we were truly considering whether God has given us instructions for how to be human, we would consider the overarching themes and philosophy God has given us.

Most people find these themes in either the Ten Commandments or Jesus's Sermon on the Mount. These both can be read like the list of how to ski in the ski instruction book: do this, don't do this. However, these instructions also happen to include the theme of why we do these things. If you want to ski, and do so well, there are some foundational issues that must be dealt with first, such as why ski in the first place? What will it do for you to ski? Also, why have enjoyments or pleasures at all? Why not just do the basics to survive? This ski book would help you figure out why you are on the mountain and what you hope to achieve; it would show you that there is an end result or purpose to the whole endeavor.

For these matters of theme and philosophy, the book of Genesis provides background context for biblical instructions—context that often gets overlooked.

In *Jesus Among Other Gods*, Ravi Zacharias points out some of the basic themes of Genesis that lay a foundation for how to be human:

> The principal thrust in the opening pages of Genesis is that God is the Creator and that He is both personal and eternal—He is a living, communicating God. The second is that the world did not come by accident, but was designed with humanity in mind—man is an intelligent, spiritual being. The third thrust is that life could not be lived out alone but through companionship—man is a relational, dependent being. The fourth aspect is that man was fashioned as a moral entity with the privilege of self-determination—man is an accountable, rational being.[15]

From these themes of man and God, we can know certain things about what it means to be human. First, we were made to be in relationship with the Being that created us. This Creator Being, this one we call "God," has communicated and is communicating with us. One of the things he communicated was that his creation of man and woman was "very good" (Genesis 1:26, 31). Humans have immeasurable value, but it doesn't come out of thin air. Our value is grounded in the value of the Creator himself, who also provided a sacrificial way to bring us out of our destructive paths and set us back aright with himself and with creation. We are not just a highly evolved animal, nor are we a random collection of atoms, nor are we a being that creates the ultimate meaning of life. Rather, we are beings that the Creator made in his own likeness, beings with a moral will, an ability to

15 Ravi Zacharias, *Jesus among Other Gods* (Nashville: Thomas Nelson, 2000), 171.

reason, and a creative bent.[16] These traits not only give humans dignity and value, but they also give us the ability to care for the rest of creation.

Second, humans were made for community. Christianity holds to monotheism, but a specific type of monotheism, namely Trinitarianism: God is one but also three.[17] He is one being consisting of three persons. He constitutes a kind of community within himself. He has made his creation to reflect this aspect of his own nature. We are a family of humans, not just individuals. As such, our instructions are to live in community with others in order to flourish as humans.

The first relationship we need is to live in fellowship with our Creator. Since God is the one who made us, there are valuable lessons, concepts, and ideas we need to learn from him. To do so, we have to recognize him for who he is and then recognize ourselves in relation to him. The second kind of community is human fellowship. As messy, heartbreaking, and downright discouraging as humans can be, we need each other. We help each other grow in ways that solitude does not. My tendencies are to draw away from people, but I learn how to more lovingly engage people who hurt me when I've been in fellowship with people and with God. I need to learn from both God and other people; otherwise, I get trapped in my own way of thinking. As I've seen

---

16 The act of creation itself implies intentionality and purpose which comes from personhood, further entailing intelligence and a will. I have included rationality in my statement of "intelligence" here. Rationality must be grounded somewhere in order for it to be a truth-making capability, as I explored in chapter 6.

17 It is not my intention here to argue for the doctrine of the Trinity. Fred Sanders, of Biola University, has written The Deep Things of God, a good place to dive into this doctrine.

from human history, a lot of devastation results when people follow their own unchecked and erroneous ways of thinking.

Third, human thoughts and actions have consequence. What I think and do does matter even if I try to believe something like ". . . as long as I'm not hurting anyone." For me, the refutation of this way of thinking goes back to the original creation and to Eve's temptation. God made a good creation, and part of that was the gift of will and of reasoning. However, Eve used her reasoning ability to rationalize something contrary to God's instructions: *God said this was the best way to interact with creation and with humans, but I think I'll do it this other way instead.* Eve's temptation, however mythologized by modern skeptics, still entails one of the main problems of humankind: the tendency to rationalize twisted desires, the corruption of our will. We try to believe we won't hurt anyone as long as we keep things to ourselves. Has not human history shown this thinking to be false? Our thoughts and actions always end up hurting others. And yet here we are in the twenty-first century still clinging to our wishful thinking on this matter.

I've discovered that in order to morally exonerate myself to follow wherever my desires lead, I must get rid of God. Yet in the process of getting rid of moral culpability, and therefore of God as the standard and judge, I lose too much. I actually lose human personhood, as I've come to see in the philosophies of the sixteenth- to twenty-first-century agnostics and atheists.

Should I believe that humans are only valuable because of what they can do and how happy they can make the rest of us? No. Are humans simply a bag of atoms, like a table or a rock, ultimately of no transcendent value? No. The only view of human beings that provides them with their proper worth is the Christian understanding. I cannot jump on the bright, shiny bandwagon of New Atheism, or even agnosticism, and deconstruct the human person. I cannot simply ski like there are no instructions, like there's no grounding for what it means to be human. But this conclusion means I have to work with what I have: a Christian commitment to a good, true, and beautiful Lord that also includes the reality of human messiness, heartbreak, and tragedy.

● CONSIDERATIONS ●

1. What is problematic about separating biological humanness from personhood?
2. Think of instances in history in which a group has been categorized as not fully human. What was the result?
3. What is one problem of assuming humans are strictly material, lacking immaterial qualities?

CHAPTER 11

NO TIDY ENDINGS

To love at all is to be vulnerable. Love anything and your heart will be wrung and possibly broken. If you want to make sure of keeping it intact you must give it to no one, not even an animal. Wrap it carefully round with hobbies and little luxuries; avoid all entanglements. Lock it up safe in the casket or coffin of your selfishness. But in that casket, safe, dark, motionless, airless, it will change. It will not be broken; it will become unbreakable, impenetrable, irredeemable. To love is to be vulnerable.

—C. S. LEWIS, *LETTERS TO MALCOLM*

"If we ever get into a healthy church situation, I'm not sure that I'll know what to do."

"What do you mean, Jo?" Roger sat across the breakfast table from me, sipping coffee. Long ago we'd established that our Wednesday mornings would be a time to "fix the world's problems" over bacon, eggs, and toast.

Before I spoke, I stared at the happy face Roger had made with my bacon and eggs on the plate. "I've lived for so long in a defensive posture against the church that I really don't know how to trust people who might actually be trustworthy. I don't know what it would take for me to trust again, specifically people in church."

"Yeah, I understand that. We've been through a lot."

"It's hard for me to see the good that's actually there because I'm so alert to the bad."

"Well, I think recognizing that issue is a good start."

"Yes, but I don't know if I even want to trust anyone anymore. I feel like it will take the resurrection to fix me. And that saddens me. This isn't the way things are supposed to be."

"I hear you, but I really don't think it's as bad as you're saying. Not everyone in the church has behaved poorly toward us, and we've learned so much from all that we've been through."

"It's not just that. Please . . . just listen." *He's always trying to fix things. I know he can't fix this one.*

Roger shot me a look that was a bit hurt but also a bit annoyed.

"I realize I've been ridiculous at times, even naive in what I've expected from the church. I've placed her on a pedestal so high and narrow that she's got nowhere to go but down. I get it. I have to deal with my idealistic tendencies. But I also know that nearly everything I've experienced is going to happen again . . . because Christians are human. They are prone to all the same problems and faults as the rest of humanity. And yet at the same time, I know people judge God and his existence on the behaviors and attitudes of those who say they follow him."

My stream-of-consciousness style of conversation was just getting going, and as usual, I took an apologetic turn.

"Don't we realize what's going on here! The alternative is that there is no God, and yet the world is still the way it is. Rape, murder, genocide, deceit, maliciousness, strife, war, starvation, disease . . . it is what it is and goes on this way until we die. To step away from any grounding for hope and then declare that I'm better off is . . . well . . . delusional."

Roger sat in silence looking at me. We had come a long way since I first started to doubt my beliefs. I had finished my master's degree in apologetics, and even obtained a university professorship, but I still struggled with the church. Roger wanted to figure out if I thought we were better or worse off from the journey I'd been on. Roger prefers a tidier answer than me. He likes to check the boxes off and scratch out the list every day—at times, an enviable trait. But I couldn't give him a tidy answer. My mind remained a mess of arguments and emotions. I didn't see an easy answer to my concerns, and nothing too promising lurked on the horizon.

I knew I should practice what I preached and give all this muddle over to God, but even knowing that God could handle my heartbrokenness and distrust still couldn't move me past twenty-four years of exploitation, shallowness, and vilification at the hands of church pastors, leaders, and members. Further complicating my confusion and sorrow was that much of what I'd experienced could appear to some people as perfectly acceptable. I was sure many people wouldn't think the things that happened to me were that bad, because even I sometimes felt that way! *I know there are people who have suffered so much more than me*, I tell myself. So I tried to convince myself that I could trust God but not his people. All the while, I knew that trusting God entailed trusting at least some of his people, or at least trusting him in situations with *people* I didn't trust.

So I am in quite a pickle, even today. I want to live in a beautiful, life-giving freedom in which I can truly love others and be loved in return. I know this will not happen perfectly in this life. However, I'm not unreceptive to the joy and light of God's love and salvation—after all, I do enjoy a loving relationship with my husband and daughter, who also happen to be "the church." And I've enjoyed the blessing of good professors and good friends who helped to restore my faith in God and in some members of the body of Christ. Still, I lack a feigned utopian positivist pipe dream (Christian, atheist, or other), a triumphalism in life. I understand that darkness is my constant companion. For in each human, I see the reflection of an indescribable beauty, and I see the destructive powers of a raging evil. This vision of humanity will not change with a shift between atheism and theism. It now remains as a burdening truth. Anyone who attempts to argue otherwise is blowing smoke.

So what are you going to do? You sound defeated.

What I am going to do is to still believe in God, but with a caveat. The answers available to me in the Christian worldview, while making the most sense of the human experience, are also going to be very messy. To reduce Christianity to a neat-and-tidy recipe for happiness is to miss it almost entirely. There are at least three reasons why this is true: (1) the arguments can only take me so far, (2) the reality of the human condition, and (3) the vision of something better entangled with our current experience.

ARGUMENTS CAN ONLY GO SO FAR

When I set out in the beginning to discover the answers to my deep questions about God and the nature of reality, I don't know exactly what I expected to find. I'm pretty sure I expected that answers would equal something like a salve for my soul. I'd find the answers and then be able to live that *victorious Christian life* (a phrase used, but not well explained, in many a sermon I've heard), or, conversely, be able to walk away from Christianity completely. Though there are many problems with my expectations of the work the arguments could do, I'll focus on a few.

First, there's always a way to view an argument as unconvincing. Arguments are based on a person's **presuppositions**. If a person does not hold to the presuppositions of the arguer, the argument can fall flat to them. Plus, if the evidence provided doesn't fit within the person's own presuppositions or even with what that person will admit as plausible, then the argument still fails to convince. It can be extremely difficult to get a person to shift one of their presuppositions.

Second, each person brings to the arguments a background of education, culture, upbringing, desires, and biases that will color what that individual sees as plausible (or even wants to see). Sir Francis Bacon in his seminal work *The New Organon* argues that it is very difficult for humans to find true knowledge based on all of these things, and more. He calls these items the idols of the mind, the obstructions to truth. After four hundred years, his work is still relevant to the problem every one of us faces when seeking true knowledge.

Presupposition: "A thing tacitly assumed beforehand at the beginning of a line of argument or course of action; the action or state of presupposing or being presupposed."* A presupposition is not something for which you argue. It is something assumed in order to make an argument.

* Lexico, s.v. "presupposition," www.lexico.com/en/definition/presupposition.

Of one thing in this clutter I am certain: I do not know how greatly my background influencers are coloring my view of things and my connection to the experiences of hurt and pain in the church. What I can do is to try to recognize *that* my background and my presuppositions *will* affect my reception of arguments for and against God's existence. In other words, I can attempt to call out my biases and then look at the arguments knowing my view is already colored. Acknowledging that I am a subject, who operates subjectively, seems to help in the process of finding what is objectively true.

Third, desires are one of the trickiest parts of argumentation to understand. I know my desires affect my understanding of church, Christians, and God. I'm not exactly sure how my desires are doing so. Therefore, I don't know exactly how to counteract my desires, nor which ones I should or should not counteract. It's a tricky thing to try to know oneself. Sometimes I wanted to leave the church community because of her hypocrisy, but other times I wanted to stick it out in church for the sake of my husband's ministry position. Desires will affect how a person sees or receives any argument and therefore whether that argument is convincing. If I want to live my life a certain way, and an argument stands in the way of my ability to live that life, I can effectively kill that argument's conclusion as a possibility for me. As I've already said, human beings can reason nearly anything they want to be true. Yet people who oppose my Christian views are rarely willing to discuss their own problematic thinking, including their desires, and how their desires potentially affect their arguments.

THE HUMAN CONDITION

It is not my intention in a few short paragraphs to delve into psychology, nor the entire history of philosophy and theology on this matter. Rather, I will speak from my own experiences. One of the life lessons I learned from church experiences is that humankind is not in good shape, and I mean to include every single individual. Right here is where I could be accused of a hasty generalization. *How do you know that humankind is not in good shape? Have you met everyone who has ever existed? No. You have not.*

I could further be accused of simply borrowing a message that sounds just like traditional Christian church teaching, and that would be partly right. Up to the point at which I went to church, I had a completely different view. I thought humankind was basically good. We all just had some hurdles to jump (from our past or our culture) in order to get to that place of peace with and respect for each other. However, my adult experience and my consideration of genocide has convincingly, and with conviction, demonstrated otherwise. Humans are drenched with the blood of their fellow man, their siblings. It is an unthinkable and irrationally grotesque situation.

My experiences with both Christians and atheists have taught me that most people are not taking this fallen status of man seriously. Outside the church, I find mocking attitudes toward this idea, built on generations of post-Enlightenment and Darwinian thinking. It seems as if we have historical amnesia that forgets that at a height of Western intelligence, ingenuity, culture, and philosophy, we still ended up creating the gas chambers of Auschwitz. Further, those who mock the idea that humans have an inherent problem are also not providing viable solutions (logically coherent or consistent) for how to teach humans to be good, toward doing good to one another. Such an attitude seems to turn a blind eye to the empirically verifiable circumstance of man's continued destruction of man, an irrationality that screams for explanation.

Inside the church community, I find inconsistency between the profession that humanity is fallen and the cautionary practices that should result from such a belief. For example, we don't pay enough attention to the problem of a fallen mind—the idea that what I believe is probably wrong much of the time. I do find, rather, many people who are easily offended if anything is stated contrary to their way of thinking. In other words, I still find people who seem to believe they are generally good and typically right. Jesus is like a good friend who did something really nice for them two thousand years ago, but it wasn't because they were so sinful. Both inside and outside the church, people don't want to recognize the truly problematic behavior and thinking of humankind. It is quite difficult to comment effectively on the human condition without adverse reactions all around.

Once I acknowledge that there is something inherently wrong with humans, I must acknowledge that I am part of that species and therefore there is something wrong with me. This idea is distasteful to our generation, causing us to aggressively search for affirmation of anything we want to do. But if it is true that humankind has chosen to do evil with the great gift of free will, and there are consequences of that abuse, then to ignore such a foundational problem or even to try to find workarounds will ultimately end in utter destruction, a savage undoing of the human species.

Part of my problem with turning away from Christianity is that I believe Christianity has the right diagnosis of the human condition, of *my* condition. Christianity has the story that makes sense of all this mess that we are in, but its story deeply and sharply daggers human pride, self-delusion, and self-aggrandizement. The picture of humanity in the story is that we are indeed fallen from our original relational status with God. The result is that our knowledge, intellect, desires, and will are affected, and as a result we constantly dehumanize ourselves and others. We are not going to be able to *pull ourselves up by our bootstraps*—or, in the language of today, just "follow our dream, speak our truth, show love not hate"—because individually we continue to be the problem. Yet Christianity also pierces the human propensity to hate ourselves. God made us in his own image, so we are of highest value (Genesis 1:26, 31). God has given us the ability to reason and a moral will. We have the capacity to do great things. And God values us so much that, rather than leave us without hope, he died to take the destructive consequence of our evil.

What I have to face in this story is my own desire, distrust, pride, and self-defense tactics—my own humanness. When I am faced with a hurtful church, it seems easier to not get emotionally entangled with others and to not use my time handling stressful situations that appear to be illogical and wrapped in another individual's selfishness. But to be involved with the church community is to risk such an entanglement. And just as I say that, I see the hypocrisy in myself. I don't want to handle the selfishness of others, but that desire is in itself selfishness on my part.

THE VISION OF SOMETHING BETTER

Two visions constantly play on my mind: the way things are and the way things should be. Most of my judgment toward the church and her hypocrisy seems to come from the entanglement of these two visions. I am holding on to a standard derived from the way things are supposed to be in order to make judgments on my church experience. But somewhere in my thoughts, I must incorporate a better understanding of the way things are and how they got that way.

I live in a post-Genesis world. One of the best descriptions of my world is found in the writings of Solomon (as I noted in the previous chapter):

Moreover, I saw under the sun that in the place of justice, even there was wickedness, and in the place of righteousness, even there was wickedness. . . . Again I saw all the oppressions that are done under the sun. And behold, the tears of the oppressed, and they had no one to comfort them! On the side of their oppressors there was power, and there was no one to comfort them. And I thought the dead who are already dead more fortunate than the living who are still alive. But better than both is he who has not yet been and has not seen the evil deeds that are done under the sun. (Ecclesiastes 3:16; 4:1–3)

Wherever Solomon should find something good, he finds its absence. In emphasizing his point, he suggests envy for the dead as well as for those who have never even lived to see all this mess caused by humanity. This is my world. It is the world in which I attend church and encounter Christians. I often fail to apply Solomon's harsh reality of a fallen world to my criticism of the church. I tend to lean toward my vision of "the way things should be" rather than see the reality of immense wreckage when fallen humans are involved.

The apostle Paul also addresses our human condition and earthly situation when he makes the comparison of "the sufferings of this present time" as being incomparable to the glory to come (Romans 8:18). Paul isn't being overly optimistic; he expounds that our "outer self is wasting away," saying that:

We are afflicted in every way, but not crushed; perplexed, but not driven to despair; persecuted, but not forsaken; struck down, but not destroyed; always carrying in the body the death of Jesus, so that the life of Jesus may also be manifested in our bodies. For we who live are always being given over

to death for Jesus' sake, so that the life of Jesus also may be
manifested in our mortal flesh. So death is at work in us, but
life in you. (2 Corinthians 4:8–12)

The wreckage and destruction are everywhere that there are
human beings. And that's a lot of devastation. I can even just
look at Paul's life. He was beaten, stoned, and left for dead while
trying to tell fellow believers in God about what God has done
for humankind. Yet Paul believed that his afflictions and perse-
cutions were not meaningless nor in vain. Instead, Paul writes
as though restoration is already here and yet is still to come: the
life of Jesus is being manifested even in suffering and death.
Paul doesn't leave his readers in the same situation as Solomon's
lament. There is hope. There is a way things should be and *will
be*. That's why Jesus is such an important part of the Christian
story. He brings hope.

When Jesus walked upon the earth, he did a lot of miracle
working, which of course caught a lot of attention, both good and
bad. Certain envious religious leaders declared that Jesus must
be working miracles through the power of Satan. Jesus answered
the illogic of their accusation and then gave an intriguing caveat:
"But if it is by the finger of God that I cast out demons, *then
the kingdom of God has come upon you*" (Luke 11:20, emphasis
added). Commentaries vary a little on what the last part of his
statement means, but it is generally agreed that Jesus is declaring that he has brought restoration to them. He has burst into
Solomon's devastated world, reversing the curse on the original
good creation. After Jesus died and rose from the dead, he confirmed his ability to bring that very kingdom of God (the right
relationship between God and his creation) into actuality.

I am truly taken by Jesus's vision. There *is* a way things

should be, and he brought it to us. In a post-Resurrection world, we have a redemptive force in our lives that can work for good, even miraculously. The world was groaning under the curse of humankind's fall (see Romans 8:22), but Jesus's resurrection was a reversal of our wreckage and the restoration of his truth and immense goodness. According to the Christian story, those who trust in Jesus for this salvation have access to that redemptive force or power through the gift of the Holy Spirit. We can be workers of incredible goodness and restoration despite our failings. This is hope. And this story matches my experience with the incredible beauty and goodness I see in humans that is juxtaposed against their forcefully tragic power to do/choose evil. It is this vision that burdens me. I want to see the redemption of Jesus lived out in his followers, demonstrating that their belief in him is real. I want to experience church members who consider the reality of Jesus and his work before they open their mouths to speak or move their bodies to act. And even as I write my plea, I know we're all going to greatly fail.

For me, this thought is of utmost importance. I'm not going to get to all the right answers, or to a complete state of peace and joy. I don't live in that world. If the Christian story is true, Jesus has victory over my evil, and yet I'm still acting out of the false knowledge and wrong desires that lead to my own death. That sounds right. It makes sense, because that matches my constant experience. Nothing I build up in my mind is ever as good as my imagination. Nothing I try to accomplish is ever as easy as I hoped. No one can fulfill me in the way I imagine, through accolades, affirmation, nor affection. It's because we all live in that post-fall of man, post-Resurrection of Jesus situation. Someday everything will be completely and finally restored, but not yet. I cannot expect the church to be untouched by Solomon's world. I further cannot expect her to live up to my expectations or vision of the way things should be.

These reasons are why I cannot give you, nor myself, a tidy ending. The answers on this side of resurrection are going to be messy. Arguments won't always get me to truth. My human condition disqualifies me from being able to save myself from falsehood and destruction. And my vision of what should be will always be entangled with what is. As I have come to a point of strong belief in God, I do see the wonderfully beautiful life that he has given me. But I also recognize the horrors of the world and am not fully at ease in my earthly home while so much evil abounds. While offering a real hope, Christianity has also, in a sense, left me heartbroken. For I imagine something that could be, and yet so often is not. I realize the world is going to continue on this heartbreaking path of hope until Hope himself returns and finalizes the restoration.

An eye-opening moment came for me when Roger told me I should take my apologetics ministry wherever people wanted it. He said, "Go where God is using you." Don't just rail against the evil in this world, constantly pushing against. Find where your work is confluent with the work of the kingdom of God. Get active in that place, working with God. His words released me from where I was stuck and gave me a much-needed reprieve. Once I began to work where God was already working in ways in which I could contribute, I saw a vast improvement in my own attitude and ability to be a force for good. Later, I began to understand how hurt I had become in church ministry with my husband. I took quite a big step back from involvement with his ministry, a much-needed retreat. Sometimes progress involves regress. Since that time, I've had years of speaking at events and teaching in churches all over the country, even though rarely in my own church. When I finished my apologetics degree, my local church did not recognize nor celebrate my graduation, but I kept writing, speaking, and attempting to figure out how God was using me for the benefit of his larger church: his kingdom.

• CONSIDERATIONS •

1. What makes it difficult to have neat and tidy answers to life's big questions?
2. Why are arguments sometimes convincing or unconvincing to people?
3. What can apologetics arguments do for people?
4. Have you ever been upset with the hypocrisy of believers? Why?

CHAPTER 12

CRASH LANDING

Jesus said, "You cannot serve two masters." At any given moment, you must choose whom you will follow. And if you choose the god of open options, you cannot at that moment choose the triune God, the one who deliberately closed off his options in order to save your life. Nothing narrows your options more than allowing your hands and feet to be nailed to a wooden cross.

—BARRY COOPER, "THE PROBLEM OF YOUR CHOICES"

So here we are. I've shared *just a little of* my hurtful experiences in the church; some of the more deeply cutting ones I have yet to share publicly (the pain of those wounds is still too near to write about it). I've thrown at you a lot of the arguments for God's existence that I've considered over the years. And I've introduced you to some of my treasured family and friends. I appreciate your sticking with me on this crazy ride.

I've discovered my naivete concerning the church and her

people. I've also discerned that in some way, I still love the church. She has absolutely broken my heart, but nevertheless I'm committed to her. I don't know exactly what that commitment will look like in the future, and I think that's okay. I'm still learning. It's important for me to know where I stand on my belief in God, on my trust in Jesus—and on my commitment to the church. I've decided to take the risk of entanglement with her. Jesus died for her. So I think I can eventually figure out how to be a part of the church in a healthy way, even knowing some horrendous jerks still haunt her ranks.

I need to learn from my past mistakes and faulty expectations. I need to be wiser and more compassionate about how I engage my fellow church humans. And instead of focusing on all the faults of the church, I need to look for people who are doing good work in the church, not idealizing them but instead being grateful for how God is using their gifts.

But what about you? What have you discovered along the way? Have you come to any conclusions, or do you maybe have a better understanding of your own experiences?

My goal was never to lead you to some predetermined conclusion. I rather had in mind that I would share with you something of an "anti-deconversion" story: the reasons why I began to doubt and the arguments that led me back around to belief. What you do with this story is really your own business. However, before we both crash-land back into our respective worlds, I will make three brazen requests, because I hope that you will sincerely take the time to think about what you believe and why you believe it.

The first request is to consider your experiences in this world in light of a broader human experience. Consider what it means to be human. To step away from Christianity is to accept a very different view of yourself and your fellow humans. If you've bought this book and you're a Christian, take some time to consider an alternative view of humanity so that you are able to understand it. What happens when you reduce humans to nothing more than animals? What happens if you believe a human is purely material matter? In those worldviews, will humans have value, purpose, and meaning? Truly take a hard look at the dignity and worth of a human once you remove the Christian worldview. Not only did a Christian view of humanity help me believe in God, it also gave me compassion for the people who were so awful to me. I'd think, *They have no idea what they are or what they were intended to be.*

God has placed the vastness of the universe within our sight as a reminder of the vastness of the interior of a single human. Yet we often treat ourselves and others as though we are simply material matter. The Christian story and its emphasis on the wreckage of sin and human evil falls flat to those who have rationalized that they are only a product of random chance reducible to material matter. The cosmic ripples generated by one wayward human soul have no meaning for those who cannot see the cosmic significance of salvation history. It was this vision of the vastness of God's creation both externally and internally that has changed my way of seeing the answers to all my questions and hurts.

Second, I want you to consider that you truly do have choices to make. Daniel Taylor's *The Skeptical Believer: Telling Stories to Your Inner Atheist* emphasizes that being skeptical is, in one way, quite the blessing, for the skeptic isn't just going to believe whatever anyone tells her. And that's wise. However, in another way, the skeptic can also become the cynic by valuing the question for the sake of the question. Taylor suggests, "Be as skeptical about skepticism as skepticism is about everything else. Skepticism should have to answer its own question about itself: 'How do you know this is true?'"[1] The cynic never lands anywhere but hovers over commitments (beliefs, relationships), holding himself just far enough away to never get really involved and just close enough to never really leave—always keeping his options open. What seems at first blush to be liberating actually ends up as enslavement to a lonely and frustrating position.

Another author describes this sort of cynicism as worshiping the "god of open options." He quotes from the story of Elijah and the contest on Mt. Carmel with the Baal worshipers.[2] In this story, the Israelites were waffling on their commitment to God. They didn't know what to believe or to whom to commit. They were keeping their options open. As the text of 1 Kings 18:21 describes, "And Elijah came near to all the people and said, 'How long will you go limping between two different opinions? If the LORD is God, follow him; but if Baal, then follow him.' And the people did not answer him a word." The people of Israel didn't realize that by not making a commitment, they were making a commitment. Though their commitment was not to God.

We are faced with choices every day to follow God or to not follow God. Sometimes those choices are overall life decisions, like whether to believe in God. Sometimes those choices are praxis commitments, like whether to act like you believe in God. But every day we do make choices, because we are rational, choice-making creatures who have free will. We're built to do so. My request is that you make those choices consciously and conscientiously. Try them out. Test-drive them. Give yourself over to your choice. Don't limp between opinions for years and years,

---

1   Daniel Taylor, *The Skeptical Believer: Telling Stories to Your Inner Atheist* (St. Paul, MN: Bog Walk, 2013), Kindle.

2   Barry Cooper, "The Problem of Your Choices," *Desiring God*, www.desiringgod .org/articles/the-problem-of-your-choices.

only to see much of your life gone without ever having made a true commitment. And try to follow your beliefs all the way out. Many people treat philosophical ideas like a smorgasbord or buffet. They'll take an atheistic foundation in their materialistic view of the sanctity of human life, but when it comes to racism, they'll grab a Christian foundation to undergird all humankind as equally valuable and dignified. It's living in logical contradiction. Don't be that guy. Try to discover what your philosophical view would mean for all the areas of your life, but especially on the big issues of human dignity and worth, what it means to be human, the problem of evil, and whether God exists.

If you are a concerted skeptic, then consider what good answers to your questions would look like. Taylor comments, "A good answer will call me to something higher, something better, perhaps something more difficult. It likely will call me to change."[3]

Finally, my third request is that you'll share your story. I am only one small voice in the vast sea of voices out there. You all have amazing stories of heartbreak and hope to share with the world. Perhaps you don't think so, but your story is as unique as you are. And your story may relate to someone who doesn't necessarily relate to my story. So would you consider sharing your own stories of belief, and why you still believe? You could start with just a one-on-one conversation, or perhaps you could post your story on social media in an article or a short video, or even share it at church. Whatever you choose, consider how to share your true story with wisdom and grace.

I do hope you will consider joining me in sharing our experiences. You see, I can communicate straight-up arguments all

---

3 Taylor, *Skeptical Believer*.

226 • WHY I STILL BELIEVE

day long—and that work *needs* to be done—but I've noticed that people who share their story with others can have a deep impact. This impact is especially true when you combine story with reasons. People want to know why you are convinced of your beliefs and how those beliefs have shaped your life. I'll pray that God will guide you and me as we speak stories of faith into a world whose philosophical foundations are falling apart.

You can share your stories with me by using #whyistillbelieve and tagging me @maryjosharp on Twitter. You can also post your stories to my Facebook page, "Why I Still Believe."

CHAPTER 1: IN THE BEGINNING WAS . . . HYPOCRISY

Books

Kinnaman, David, and Gabe Lyons. *UnChristian: What a New Generation Really Thinks about Christianity . . . and Why It Matters.*

Wright, Bradley R. E. *Christians are Hate-Filled Hypocrites . . . and Other Lies You've Been Told.*

Wright, N. T. *After You Believe: Why Christian Character Matters.*

Articles

"Hypocrisy Is Keeping People from the Church—an Excerpt from *The Problem of God.*" https://zondervanacademic.com/blog/hypocrisy-is-keeping-people-from-the-church-an-excerpt-from-the-problem-of-god.

CHAPTER 2: WEARING THE WRONG CLOTHING

Books

Boyd, Gregory. *Benefit of the Doubt* (specifically on certainty of beliefs).

Conway, Bobby. *Doubting toward Faith.*

Habermas, Gary. *Dealing with Doubt* (fully available online).

———. *The Risen Jesus and Future Hope.*

Habermas, Gary. *The Thomas Factor* (fully available online). www.garyhabermas.com/books/thomas_factor/thomas_factor.htm.

Habermas, Gary, and Michael Licona. *The Case for the Resurrection of Jesus.*

Ortberg, John. *Faith and Doubt.*

Strobel, Lee. *The Case for a Creator.*

Stump, J. B., et al. *Four Views on Creation, Evolution, and Intelligent Design.*

Articles

Ortberg, John. "Can You Doubt Too Much? An Interview with John Ortberg." https://fulleryouthinstitute.org/articles/can-you-doubt -too-much-an-interview-with-john-ortberg.

Powell, Kara, and Brad M. Griffin. "I Doubt It: Making Space for Hard Questions." https://fulleryouthinstitute.org/articles/i-doubt-it.

CHAPTER 3: GOD, ARE YOU THERE?

Books

Craig, William Lane. *On Guard.*

———. *Reasonable Faith.*

Craig, William Lane, and Paul Copan, eds. *Come Let Us Reason.*

———. *Contending with Christianity's Critics.*

Dembski, William, and Michael Licona, eds. *Evidence for God.*

Moreland, J. P. *Christianity and the Nature of Science.*

Rea, Michael C. *The Hiddenness of God.*

Ross, Hugh. *The Creator and the Cosmos.*

Strobel, Lee. *The Case for a Creator.*

Articles and Videos

Craig, William Lane. "The Kalam Cosmological Argument." https:// youtu.be/6CulBuMCLg0.

———. "In What Sense Is It Impossible for the Universe to Come from Nothing?" www.biola.edu/blogs/good-book-blog/2017/in-what -sense-is-it-impossible-for-the-universe-to-come-from-nothing.

———. "Objections to the Existence of God: Divine Hiddenness." https://youtu.be/d8EZBX8ZbWQ.

——. "Who Designed the Designer?" www.reasonablefaith.org/ videos/lectures/who-designed-the-designer.

Craig, William Lane, and Austin Dacey. "Does God Exist?" www .youtube.com/watch?v=pnof3-hdMOE.

Craig, William Lane, and Kevin Harris. "A Universe from Nothing." www.reasonablefaith.org/media/reasonable-faith-podcast/a -universe-from-nothing/.

Lennox, John. "Stephen Hawking and God." www.rzim.org/read/just -thinking-magazine/stephen-hawking-and-god.

Licona, Michael. "Out of Nothing, Nothing Comes." www.bethinking .org/is-there-a-creator/ex-nihilo-nihil-fit-out-of-nothing-nothing -comes.

Moser, Paul K. "Divine Hiddenness, Death, and Meaning." http:// pmoser.sites.luc.edu/idolanon/Divine%20Hiddenness,%20 Death,%20and%20Meaning.pdf.

Wallace, J. Warner. "God's Hiddenness Is Intended to Provoke Us." https://coldcasechristianity.com/writings/gods-hiddenness-is -intended-to-provoke-us/.

Zacharias, Ravi. "The Hiddenness of God." www.rzim.org/watch/the -hiddenness-of-god.

CHAPTER 4: RESURRECTION

Books

Copan, Paul, ed. *Will the Real Jesus Please Stand Up? A Debate between William Lane Craig and John Dominic Crossan*.

Evans, Craig. *Fabricating Jesus*.

Geivett, Douglas, and Gary Habermas. *In Defense of Miracles*.

Habermas, Gary. *The Risen Jesus and Future Hope*.

Habermas, Gary, and Michael Licona. *The Case for the Resurrection*.

Komoszewski, Ed, James Sawyer, and Daniel Wallace. *Reinventing Jesus*.

Lewis, C. S. *Miracles*.

Licona, Michael. *Paul Meets Muhammad: A Christian-Muslim Debate on the Resurrection*.

Strobel, Lee. *The Case for Christ.*
———. *The Case for Easter.*

Articles and Videos

Craig, William Lane. "Jesus' Resurrection." www.reasonablefaith.org/writings/scholarly-writings/historical-jesus/jesus-resurrection/.

Gleghorn, Michael. "Ancient Evidence for Jesus from Non-Christian Sources by Michael Gleghorn." www.bethinking.org/jesus/ancient-evidence-for-jesus-from-non-christian-sources.

Hutchinson, Ian. "Can a Scientist Believe in the Resurrection?" www.veritas.org/can-scientist-believe-resurrection-three-hypotheses/.

Licona, Michael. Many videos and articles on his website, Risen Jesus. www.risenjesus.com.

McGrath, Alister. "The Resurrection." www.bethinking.org/resurrection/the-resurrection.

Zukeran, Patrick. "The Resurrection—Fact or Fiction?" www.bethinking.org/did-jesus-rise-from-the-dead/the-resurrection-fact-or-fiction.

CHAPTER 5: LESSONS FROM A SOCIOPATH AND AN EX-MUSLIM

Books

Marshall, Paul, Roberta Green, and Lela Gilbert. *Islam at the Crossroads.*
Qureshi, Nabeel. *Answering Jihad.*
———. *No God But One: Allah or Jesus?*
———. *Seeking Allah, Finding Jesus.*
Samples, Kenneth. *God Among Sages.*
Zacharias, Ravi. *Jesus among Other Gods.*
———. *Light in the Shadow of Jihad.*

Articles and Videos

Petersen, Jonathan. "How Friendship Helped a Follower of Islam See the Truth about Jesus." www.biblegateway.com/blog/2018/08/how-friendship-helped-a-follower-of-islam-see-the-truth-about-jesus/.

Qureshi, Nabeel. "Crossing Over: An Intellectual and Spiritual Journey from Islam to Christianity." www.answering-islam.org/Authors/Qureshi/testimony.htm.

———. "Seeking Allah, Finding Jesus, an interview with Nabeel Qureshi." https://youtu.be/NGJzkm8lZjU.

———. "Who Was Jesus-Qureshi vs. Qureshi-01-Nabeel's Opening Statement." https://youtu.be/p53zR_7Q1m4.

———. "Why I Stopped Believing Islam Is a Religion of Peace." www.premierchristianradio.com/Shows/Saturday/The-Profile/Videos/Why-I-stopped-believing-Islam-is-a-religion-of-peace-Nabeel-Qureshi.

———. "Why I Stopped Believing Islam Is a Religion of Peace." https://youtu.be/2htOWOF4gqs.

Roys, Julie. "Do Muslims & Christians Worship the Same God?: An Interview with Former Muslim Nabeel Qureshi, Part One." http://julieroys.com/do-muslims-christians-worship-the-same-god-an-interview-with-former-muslim-nabeel-qureshi-part-one/.

———. "Interview: Former Muslim Nabeel Qureshi on "Is Islam a Religion of Peace? (Part 2)." www.christianpost.com/news/former-muslim-nabeel-qureshi-islam-religion-of-peace-interview.html.

Wood, David. "Is Islam a Religion of Peace?" https://youtu.be/DwrbBuIbjnM.

———. "What Is Islam?" www.answeringmuslims.com/2013/07/what-is-islam.html.

———. "Why I Am a Christian (David Wood, Former Atheist's Conversion Testimony)." https://youtu.be/DakEcY7Z5GU.

CHAPTER 6: DEBATING GOOD AND EVIL

Books

Hart, David Bentley. *The Doors of the Sea*.

Jones, Clay. *Why Does God Allow Evil?*

Keller, Timothy. *Walking with God through Pain and Suffering*.

Lewis, C. S. *A Grief Observed*.

———. *The Problem of Pain*.

Meister, Chad, and Paul Moser, eds. *The Cambridge Companion to the Problem of Evil*.

Zacharias, Ravi, and Vince Vitale. *Why Suffering?*

Articles and Videos

Craig, William Lane. "The Problem of Evil." www.reasonablefaith .org/writings/popular-writings/existence-nature-of-god/the -problem-of-evil/.

———. "Suffering and Evil: The Logical Problem." https://youtu.be/ k64YJYBUFLM.

———. "Suffering and Evil: The Probability Version." https://youtu .be/cxj8ag8Ntd4.

Craig, William Lane, and Walter-Sinnott Armstrong. "Do Evil and Suffering Disprove God?" www.reasonablefaith.org/media/ debates/do-evil-and-suffering-disprove-god/.

DeWitt, Dan. "Atheism and the Problem of Evil." www.crossway.org/ articles/atheism-and-the-problem-of-evil/.

Jordan, Stephen S. "C. S. Lewis and Eight Reasons for Believing in Objective Morality." www.moralapologetics.com/wordpress/ 2019/1/18/c-s-lewis-and-8-reasons-for-believing-in-objective -morality.

Koukl, Greg. "Bosnia, Rape, and the Problem of Evil by Greg Koukl." www.bethinking.org/suffering/bosnia-rape-and-the -problem-of-evil.

Sharp, Mary Jo. "Addressing the Emotional Problem of Evil: Why Christians Hope." www.equip.org/article/addressing-emotional -problem-evil-christians-hope/.

———. "August Apologetics: Mary Jo Sharp on the Problem of Evil."
https://youtu.be/EZCZOhCv9Go.
Wallace, J. Warner. "The Problem with Answering the Problem of
Evil." https://coldcasechristianity.com/writings/the-problem-with
-answering-the-problem-of-evil/.

CHAPTER 7: PRINCE OF PEACE OR POSER

Books
Beilby, James K., and Paul Rhodes Eddy, eds. *The Historical Jesus:
Five Views.*
Foreman, Mark. "Challenging the *Zeitgeist* Movie: Parallelomania
on Steroids." In *Come Let Us Reason: New Essays in Christian
Apologetics*, edited by William Lane Craig and Paul Copan.
Holding, J. P. *Shattering the Christ Myth.*
Nash, Ronald. *The Gospel and the Greeks: Did the New Testament
Borrow from Pagan Thought?*
Oswalt, John N. *The Bible Among the Myths.*
Porter, Stanley E., and Stephen J. Bedard. *Unmasking the Pagan
Christ: An Evangelical Response to the Cosmic Christ Idea.*
Sharp, Mary Jo. "Does the Story of Jesus Mimic Pagan Mystery
Stories?" In *Come Let Us Reason: New Essays in Christian
Apologetics*, edited by William Lane Craig and Paul Copan.
———. "Is the Story of Jesus Borrowed from Pagan Myths?" In *In
Defense of the Bible*, edited by Terry Wilder and Steve Cowan.

Articles and Videos
Licona, Michael. "The Christ Conspiracy." www.bethinking.org/
is-christianity-true/the-christ-conspiracy.
———. "Did the Early Christians Borrow the Idea of Jesus's
Resurrection from Pagan Myths?" www.risenjesus.com/early
-christians-borrow-idea-jesuss-resurrection-pagan-myths.
Sharp, Mary Jo. "Is Jesus a Myth?" http://apologeticsguy.com/2011/07/
is-jesus-a-myth-mithras-osiris-theory-christianity/.

———. "Jesus and Pagan Mythology." https://youtu.be/Zb4cMs52-vk.

———. "Resurrection Myths vs. Resurrection of Jesus—Mithras." http://confidentchristianity.com/?p=293.

———. "Resurrection Myths vs. Resurrection of Jesus—Osiris." http://confidentchristianity.com/?p=296.

———. "Resurrection Myths vs. Resurrection of Jesus—Tammuz and Adonis." http://confidentchristianity.com/?p=298.

———. "Was Christianity Copied from Pagan Myth?" https://youtu.be/WD-SJx7-66s.

———. "Zeitgeist, the Movie—Christianity versus the Pagan Mystery Religions." http://confidentchristianity.com/?p=289.

Yamauchi, Edwin M. "Easter: Myth, Hallucination, or History?" www.leaderu.com/everystudent/easter/articles/yama.html.

Wallace, J. Warner. "Why the Pre-Jesus Mythologies Fail to Prove Jesus Is a Myth." https://coldcasechristianity.com/writings/why-the-pre-jesus-mythologies-fail-to-prove-jesus-is-a-myth/.

CHAPTER 8: A CONCERNING VOID

Books

Bannister, Andy. The Atheist Who Didn't Exist: Or the Dreadful Consequences of Bad Arguments.

Beckwith, Francis, and Gregory Koukl. Relativism: Feet Firmly Planted in Mid-Air.

Budziszewski, J. What We Can't Not Know.

Chesterton, G. K. Orthodoxy.

Geisler, Norman, and Frank Turek. I Don't Have Enough Faith to Be an Atheist.

Lewis, C. S. The Abolition of Man.

———. Mere Christianity.

McGrath, Alister. The Twilight of Atheism.

Schaeffer, Francis. How Should We Then Live?

Zacharias, Ravi. The End of Reason.

Articles and Videos

Barnett, Tim. "Four Problems with Evolutionary Morality." www.str
.org/article/four-problems-evolutionary-morality.

Craig, William Lane. "The Absurdity of Life without God" www
.reasonablefaith.org/writings/popular-writings/existence-nature
-of-god/the-absurdity-of-life-without-god/.

———. "Can Atheists Trust Their Own Minds?" https://youtu.be/
byN38dyZb-k.

———. "Can We Be Good without God?" www.reasonablefaith.org/
writings/popular-writings/existence-nature-of-god/can-we-be
-good-without-god/.

Copan, Paul. "The Moral Argument for God's Existence." www
.namb.net/apologetics-blog/the-moral-argument-for-gods
-existence/.

Galloway, Katie. "Reclaiming Reason from Atheism." www
.bethinking.org/atheism/reclaiming-reason-from-atheism.

Lennox, John. "John Lennox Busts a Myth about Religion, Faith and
Science." www.solas-cpc.org/john-lennox-busts-a-myth-about
-religion-faith-and-science/.

Meister, Chad. "Atheists and the Quest for Objective Morality." www
.equip.org/article/atheists-and-the-quest-for-objective-morality/.

Richards, Jay W. "C. S. Lewis and the Argument from Reason."
https://evolutionnews.org/2013/11/cs_lewis_and_th/.

Wood, David. "What Is the Argument from Reason?" www.acts17
.net/2012/12/what-is-argument-from-reason.html.

CHAPTER 9: THE PROBLEM OF BEAUTY

Books

Baggett, David, Gary R. Habermas, Jerry L. Wall, eds. *C. S. Lewis as
Philosopher: Truth, Goodness, and Beauty.*

Lewis, C. S. *The Weight of Glory.*

Markos, Louis. *Restoring Beauty.*

Pearcey, Nancy. *Saving Leonardo.*

236 • WHY I STILL BELIEVE

Rookmaaker, H. R. *Modern Art and the Death of a Culture.*

Ryken, Leland. *The Liberated Imagination: Thinking Christianly About the Arts.*

Schaeffer, Francis A. *Art and the Bible.*

———. *The Complete Works of Francis A. Schaeffer: Volume Three, A Christian View of Spirituality.*

———. *How Should We Then Live?: The Rise and Decline of Western Thought and Culture.*

Scruton, Roger. *Beauty.*

———. *Beauty: A Very Short Introduction.*

Tallon, Phil. "The Theistic Argument from Beauty and Play." In *Two Dozen or So Arguments for God's Existence*, edited by Jerry Walls and Trent Doughtery.

Articles and Videos

Colson, Chuck. "Chuck Colson on Art, Worship, and the Bible." www.breakpoint.org/2017/07/made-for-beauty-2/.

Fellows, Andrew. "Recovering Goodness, Beauty and Truth." www.labri.org/england/resources/05052008/AF02_Goodness_Beauty_3E64FE.pdf.

Ortlund, Ray. "Something Profound in Our Generation." www.thegospelcoalition.org/blogs/ray-ortlund/something-profound-in-our-generation/.

Reynolds, John Mark. "Beauty and the Destruction of the Individual." https://youtu.be/61kVY3OuePw.

———. "Beauty and the Existence of God." https://www.patheos.com/blogs/eidos/2017/06/beauty-existence-god/.

Scruton, Roger. "Beauty and Desecration." www.city-journal.org/html/beauty-and-desecration-13172.html.

———. "Roger Scruton: The Good, the True, and the Beautiful." https://youtu.be/10PG8VZiZaQ.

———. "Why Beauty Matters by Roger Scruton." http://americandigest.org/wp/beauty-matters-roger-scruton/. (Please note that some images and audio in the discussion of art are inappropriate for young audiences.)

Zubia, Aaron, and the Summit Staff. "The Aesthetic: Clues to God's Design for Beauty." www.summit.org/resources/articles/the -aesthetic-clues-to-gods-design-for-beauty/.

CHAPTER 10: INSTRUCTIONS ON HOW TO BE HUMAN

Books

Bloom, Allan. *The Closing of the American Mind.*
Koukl, Gregory. *The Story of Reality.*
McGrath, Alister. *The Dawkins Delusion.*
———. *The Twilight of Atheism.*
Moreland, J. P. *Love God with All Your Mind.*
———. *Scaling the Secular City.*
Zacharias, Ravi. *Can Man Live without God.*

Articles and Videos

Bannister, Andy. "What Does It Really Mean to Be Human?" www .rzim.org/read/a-slice-of-infinity/what-does-it-really-mean-to-be -human.
Craig, William Lane. "Is There Meaning to Life?" https://youtu.be/ NKGnXgH_CzE.
Klusendorf, Scott. "Peter Singer's Bold Defense of Infanticide." www .equip.org/article/peter-singers-bold-defense-of-infanticide/.
Sullivan, Dennis M. "Defending Human Personhood: Some Insights from Natural Law." www.cedarville.edu/~/media/Files/PDF/ Center-for-Bioethics/personhood_and_natural_law.pdf.
Wyatt, John. "What Is a Person?" www.cmf.org.uk/resources/ publications/content/?context=article&id=684.
Zacharias, Ravi. "Origin, Meaning, Morality, and Destiny." www .ligonier.org/learn/conferences/defending-the-faith-2018-west -coast-conference/origin-meaning-morality-destiny/.

CHAPTER 11: NO TIDY ENDINGS

Books

Lewis, C. S. *Surprised by Joy.*

Moreland, J. P., and Klaus Issler. *In Search of a Confident Faith: Overcoming Barriers to Trusting in God.*

Stetzer, Ed. *Christians in the Age of Outrage.*

Taylor, Daniel. *The Myth of Certainty.*

———. *The Skeptical Believer: Telling Stories to Your Inner Atheist.*

Willard, Dallas. *The Divine Conspiracy.*

Wright, R. E. *Christians Are Hate-Filled Hypocrites . . . and Other Lies You've Been Told.*

Articles

Groothuis, Douglas. "A Royal Ruin: Pascal's Argument from Humanity to Christianity." www.bethinking.org/christian-beliefs/a-royal-ruin.

Roberts, Tom. "Where Can We Find Lasting Happiness?" www.bethinking.org/is-there-meaning-to-life/where-find-happiness.

Taylor, Justin. "The Purpose of Paul's Suffering: To Mediate Christ's Resurrection Life." www.thegospelcoalition.org/blogs/justin-taylor/the-purpose-of-pauls-suffering-to-mediate-christs-resurrection-life/.

CHAPTER 12: CRASH LANDING

Books

Copan, Paul. *A Little Book for New Philosophers.*

———. *True for You, But Not for Me.*

———. *That's Just Your Interpretation.*

Keller, Timothy. *Making Sense of God.*

———. *The Reason for God: Belief in an Age of Skepticism.*

Pearcey, Nancy. *Finding Truth.*

Sire, James. *The Universe Next Door.*

Stokes, Mitch. *A Shot of Faith to the Head: Be a Confident Believer in an Age of Cranky Atheists.*

APOLOGETICS WEBSITES

Be Thinking Ministries: www.bethinking.org
Come Reason Ministries: www.comereason.org
Confident Christianity (that's me): www.confidentchristianity.com
Cross-Examined Ministries (Frank Turek): www.crossexamined.org
C. S. Lewis Institute: www.cslewisinstitute.org
David Wood YouTube channel: www.youtube.com/user/
    Acts17Apologetics
Discovery Institute: www.discovery.org
Gary Habermas website: www.garyhabermas.com
Jude 3 Project: www.jude3project.com
L'Abri Fellowship: http://labri.org
Life Training Institute: https://prolifetraining.com
Mama Bear Apologetics: https://mamabearapologetics.com
Moral Apologetics: www.moralapologetics.com
Nancy Pearcey website: www.nancypearcey.com
Paul Copan website: www.paulcopan.com
Ravi Zacharias International Ministries: www.rzim.org
Reasonable Faith Ministries (William Lane Craig):
    www.reasonablefaith.org
Reasons to Believe: www.rtb.org
Risen Jesus Ministries (Michael Licona): www.risenjesus.com
Society of G. K. Chesterton: www.chesterton.org
Solas Center for Public Christianity: www.solas-cpc.org
Stand to Reason Ministries: www.str.org
William Dembski website: https://billdembski.com